finding mary

finding
mary

ONE FAMILY'S JOURNEY ON THE
ROAD TO AUTISM RECOVERY

RANDY ROBERTSON

iUniverse, Inc.
New York   Bloomington

Finding Mary
One Family's Journey on the Road to Autism Recovery

iUniverse books may be ordered through booksellers or by contacting:

iUniverse
1663 Liberty Drive
Bloomington, IN 47403
www.iuniverse.com
1-800-Authors (1-800-288-4677)

Because of the dynamic nature of the Internet, any Web addresses or links contained in this book may have changed since publication and may no longer be valid. The views expressed in this work are solely those of the author and do not necessarily reflect the views of the publisher, and the publisher hereby disclaims any responsibility for them.

ISBN: 978-1-4502-2302-7 (sc)
ISBN: 978-1-4502-2303-4 (ebk)

Printed in the United States of America

iUniverse rev. date: 04/20/2010

Foreword

Those of us who are health professionals in the middle of an epidemic are aware that statistics are composed of individuals. As a physician working with autistic children I have met many of these individuals and their parents and I've been humbled by these encounters. Physicians are always learning from their patients and I have learned from Mary. Now, with this book, I've also been taught by her father.

At our health center, we believe that most chronic health challenges are not discreet entities with single causes, but are rather a spectrum of disorders affecting individuals and are due to a variety of imbalances, allergies, infections, toxicities and genetic susceptibilities. The Autism Spectrum Disorders are perfect examples of this concept.

Medical science is offering some information which is helping us sort through the puzzle of autism, but ultimately we are dealing with individuals, people like Mary, with their own unique combination of metabolic, environmental and genetic factors. We have to play hunches and do a fair amount of "trial and error." So it is due to the courage and effort of people like the Robertsons that we gain the experience to help others.

This book also demonstrates the importance of working with the full range of specialists and therapists that are so essential for good outcomes. We feel our metabolic work enables the child's brain to better absorb the interventions of the speech and occupational therapists. Physical therapists, nutritionists, teachers and neurologists all have special roles in the care of these children.

Ultimately, however, it boils down to the parents. The Robertsons had to deal with all the uncertainties and questions that exist in this field. They had to navigate the websites, absorb conflicting advice and direct the entire process. When a child has a heart valve problem or scoliosis, there are wise specialists who can carry the burden of knowledge and supervision. In autism, it's the parents who need to run the show and make the tough choices. They're the ones who have to fight for services and advocate for their child. They're the experts.

This book tells the story of one family. It's a personal journey as all these journeys are, but it generously points out a path that others may choose to follow.

By Dr. Michael Compain, M.D.
Rhinebeck Health Center, NY

This book is dedicated to beautiful Mary Robertson, who inspires, amuses and challenges her family every day. It is also dedicated to the incredible team of people – including family, friends and professionals – who have helped Mary on her road to autism recovery the past five years.

Special thanks to my wife, Debby Robertson, for her support and editing skills, both of which helped make this book a reality. Also special thanks to my brother, Bud Robertson, for his meticulous manuscript editing and photo preparations.

TABLE OF CONTENTS

Introduction

There are far too many families traveling the road to autism recovery these days. As many as 1 in 110 children are diagnosed with autism spectrum disorders, according to a report from the Centers for Disease Control and Prevention in December, 2009.[1] That alarming ratio has been worsening for years, to the point that we are in the midst of a major crisis early in this century.

People with autism exhibit various traits depending on the severity of their condition. These can include: lack of eye contact, hand flapping, poor or no social skills, sparse or no language, picky eating, difficulty transitioning from one activity to another, obsessions with a specific object or subject and an inclination to throw horrific tantrums if they don't get what they want when they want it.

My daughter Mary was diagnosed with autism in 2005 and she demonstrated all of those characteristics at one time or another. Mary is now 8, and some of the traits still surface from time to time, even as we proceed further and further along the road to autism recovery.

We feel quite fortunate that Mary responded well to many treatments. She is what is often called "high-functioning" in the autism community. She can dress and feed herself, she speaks, albeit not in long or detailed conversations, she's toilet trained, can read books, plays the piano with two hands and shows warmth and feelings toward others on a regular basis.

But it wasn't always that way. For years Mary threw world-class tantrums, refused to use the toilet, ignored everybody completely and lived in a fantasy world inhabited only by her and a select group of television cartoon characters. It was sad and maddening at the same time.

My wife Debby and I were perplexed and overwhelmed as we researched autism spectrum disorders and frantically looked for help. We quickly learned there was no cure for autism, and not only that, the treatments being discussed online and in our community were often challenged by others as being ineffective or even dangerous. There were conflicting reports on just about every type of treatment, including the gluten-free, casein-free diet, hyperbaric oxygen therapy, chelation, toxin cleanses, over-the-counter supplements, prescription drugs and so on.

We initially steered clear of the biomedical options and focused on behavioral therapy provided through the school system. After some initial success Mary hit a plateau, at which time we moved forward with a doctor who opened our eyes to the many possibilities of biomedical therapy.

Under the careful watch and guidance of Michael Compain, M.D. of the Rhinebeck Health Center in upstate New York, we embraced many cutting-edge and off-label treatments. Dr. Compain and other members of the Defeat Autism Now! organization advocate biomedical strategies that have been found to lessen symptoms in many autistic patients. Many of these strategies are not widely accepted by traditional medical doctors because they have yet to be approved by the Food and Drug Administration as safe and effective in treating autism spectrum disorders specifically. Nevertheless, they often work quite well, we found. Though several of these treatments proved ineffective, and even worsened Mary's condition temporarily, in the long run they proved to be highly effective and rapidly increased the pace of Mary's on-going recovery.

(Please consult your physician before starting any new treatment program for yourself or your children. Mary's treatments are mentioned here and later in the book for educational purposes only. The author has no

medical training, or affiliation with the Defeat Autism Now! organization or the Rhinebeck Health Center, except as a parent of a patient at the Rhinebeck Health Center.)

Mary's exceptional recovery is the result of hours, days, weeks, months and years of perseverance, trying just about every treatment option imaginable as well as working closely with outstanding teachers and therapists. We also envision Mary completely recovered and never waver in our belief that she will lead a long and productive life. We constantly remind ourselves to stay positive and believe in the ultimate outcome. In the song "Walk On," the rock band U2 sings of a place that has to be believed to be seen. That's how we feel about our journey with Mary. We *believe* she will recover completely and soon, now we just have to get to that place.

While we remain optimistic and believing, raising an autistic child is nevertheless in many ways like caring for a 3-year-old indefinitely, even with all the progress Mary has made. There are still too often those moments that cause your blood to boil or your heart to skip a beat. While Mary can sit and read a book, she can't pick up many basic social cues and determine appropriate public behavior. She also tends to do whatever she wants, when she wants — the mindset of a 3-year-old — which can be frustrating for all. For example, in the past year, when she was 7, Mary:

- Wandered off on her own at the park when the rest of the family was playing together, because she decided she was ready to go home, never bothering to tell anyone she was heading out;
- Sprayed shaving cream all over the bathroom sink and mirror at her piano teacher's apartment because it looked fun;
- Opened her mother's make-up bag and rubbed make-up all over the bedspread, mirror and dresser for reasons known only to her;

- Screamed at the top of her lungs "different shirt, different shirt" about a dozen times at the swimming pool club when the only dry shirt we brought was a tank top that she didn't feel like wearing that day.

Most people expect more of a 7-year-old, but with autism it's a mixed bag every day. She can act 7 or 3 or anywhere in between on any given day and minute.

Fortunately there's never been a better time to confront autism, because public awareness is at an all-time high and increasing. Celebrities and media personalities are focusing on autism and money is being raised worldwide in the hopes of discovering a medical breakthrough to cure autism. The Autism Speaks organization is raising millions of dollars each year through its walks and special events, money that is being used to fund research and raise awareness.

The reality is that nobody knows what causes autism and why children are affected in so many different ways. Some people attribute the rise in autism to vaccines, others believe it may be genetic, still others think it is the result of the increasing level of toxins in our water, air and food. Truth is nobody knows — and as a result, for now, there is no cure, just that long road to a possible recovery that may or may not ever be reached. Even those who reach the destination and are considered recovered are said to occasionally show quirky elements of their past, so the term "recovered" is used instead of "cured" because to be cured suggests there are no remaining traces of the condition.

As we progressed on our journey along the road to autism recovery, Mary emerged a little at a time. She opened our eyes to people, places and things we never knew existed. An amazing thing happened along the way: each time we pursued a lead or changed directions, another incredible person came into our lives.

This book is about Mary and those special people who are part of the journey to reclaim Mary, with all of her quirkiness and all of the challenges and leaps of faith along the way. It's about how a healthy and happy young girl could so quickly and completely regress that she seemingly lost all ability to speak and interact with even her own parents. It's about how a family pulls together in a slow-motion crisis. It's about the beautiful and wonderful people in the world who are working every day with special-needs children such as Mary and making a real difference. It's about faith and the belief that all obstacles can be overcome with enough prayers, determination and positive affirmation.

Truly there is something about this Mary, whose light is shining more brightly each day. As we travel the road together, she's now reading the highway signs, beginning to question where we're going, and finally showing enthusiasm and awareness that we're on a journey together.

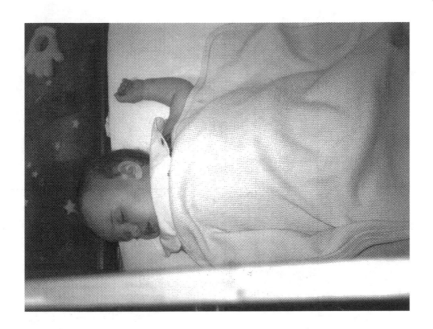

1. A Beautiful Beginning

Before this journey began, before we dedicated our lives to finding Mary, we enjoyed a truly special time. For the first two years of her life, Mary charmed and loved and delighted everyone around her. She sang and danced and talked and hugged and laughed. *She interacted*. She wore cute little pink outfits, ribbons in her hair, shiny black Mary Jane shoes, whatever her mother wanted. It was marvelous and wonderful and I have the video to prove it.

Roll the tape and there's Mary, just past her second birthday in December 2003. She was the queen of our little house and she let everyone know it. There's Mary decorating the Christmas tree, at least as well as a toddler can. She reaches in a box, picks up an ornament and manages to hook it on a low tree branch. There's her smile, and how proud she looks! Now she's smiling at the video camera – she knows I'm recording this event. Next, she picks up a play telephone.

"Talk on the phone, Daddy," Mary requests playfully.

She looks me right in the eyes and waves the phone toward me, beckoning me to play with her. Mary is engaging and entertaining. Her brown hair flows past her shoulders, all full of natural curls. Her eyes, so blue at birth, are gradually turning a beautiful hazel color. She clearly has her Grandmother Robertson's nose, a smallish rounded nose with a slight upturn at the end. So cute and adorable, and Mary has the personality to complement her beauty. I look over at my wife Debby who is busy hanging decorations, and I smile.

"I'm living the American dream," I thought to myself as I shut off the video camera and rushed over to play with little Mary.

At that point Debby, Mary and I really were living in a dream world. The nightmare of autism hadn't overtaken our lives yet. We were happily settled into a modest middle-class home in Queens, New York. The house, built in 1920, looked like so many others in Queens with its small green lawn in front, brick stoop leading to the front door and the standard three bedrooms and 1½ bathrooms inside. The house had white vinyl siding, a huge bay window in front and a charcoal gray roof on top.

Debby and I bought the house in 2000 after relocating from Chicago. We initially rented an apartment nearby while we looked around for just the right home and neighborhood. We found exactly what we were looking for in Whitestone, a predominantly Italian and Greek neighborhood in the northeast corner of Queens. It's a safe and pleasant place to raise a family, and conveniently close to work in Manhattan.

When Debby and I bought the house, we brought along our dogs, black cocker spaniel mutts named Xena and Diva. And we planned to start a family, perhaps a few years down the road. One neighbor smiled when I mentioned our plans, quickly suggesting that we'd have a baby inside a year and would soon fill the house. I shrugged and chuckled at the thought, but he was right. By spring of 2001 Debby's belly was bulging and little Mary was soon to join the world.

Debby's pregnancy was a fun and exciting time for both of us. We read lots of books about motherhood and fatherhood and scanned through a half-dozen baby name books. The pregnancy itself was normal, no problems or scares along the way. Debby was careful about what she ate and followed a light workout routine to stay as fit as possible.

The big day came September 26, 2001 when Mary was born at 3 a.m. The onset of labor to Mary's birth took only two hours, and Mary entered the world without complications. Everything about Mary looked perfect that day, and I distinctly remember holding my newborn baby girl and saying to myself that I would always do everything in my power to make Mary the happiest, safest and most loved child in the world.

2. The Day-Care Cough

Ten weeks after Mary was born, we began dropping her off at a day-care center just 15 minutes from home. Debby and I went back to work full-time, and though we missed Mary terribly, we were both committed to being successful in our jobs. I had completed my MBA at DePaul University in Chicago less than two years prior and had grand professional aspirations. I was doing well in my job at a consulting firm, managing an international team of approximately 200 graphic designers from my office in midtown Manhattan. Debby kept busy racing up the corporate ladder at a large national bank. Throughout Debby's pregnancy we scouted local day-care centers, looking for just the right place for our precious Mary.

The day-care center we chose was newly built with bright lights, fresh paint, a landscaped yard, security cameras, ample parking and a warm environment. The first few days we were emotional about leaving Mary in someone else's hands, but that worry quickly went away as we got used to the routine. Those were long days for Mary at the center, arriving at 7:30 a.m. and staying until I picked her up at 6 p.m. We rationalized that Mary was sleeping half the day anyway, and we were busy earning money to pay off our house, putting money away for Mary's college education, etc.

Unfortunately, almost from the beginning Mary began to get sick quite a bit. This was common among infants in day-care centers we were told because the germs spread so easily. Not to worry we were told. "Let her build up her immunities now, so by the time she enters school she'll have had everything already and won't miss school then," was a regular comment we heard from other parents of children in day-care. That argument did make some sense, but unfortunately Mary was struggling quite often to stay healthy. Though we didn't realize it at the time, it was likely that Mary's immune system wasn't very strong.

That first winter, when Mary was only four-months old, she developed a deep cough and labored to breathe. We pulled out the baby medical books, which suggested holding her near a hot shower so she could breathe the humid vapors. But Mary wasn't getting better, and the pediatrician diagnosed her with bronchiolitis and recommended a nebulizer.

"A what?" I asked. "What the heck is a nebulizer?"

The doctor, a kind and humorous gentleman with gray hair and a quiet confidence about him, explained that a nebulizer is a small machine into which we would pour liquid medicine. The nebulizer would then produce a mist full of that medicine which Mary would breathe directly. The result was that Mary inhaled the medicine via the mist directly and deeply into her lungs, and the medicine helped relax the muscles and open her airways.

We picked up the prescription for a medicine called Albuterol[2] and got out the nebulizer. It just about broke our hearts to have to use the thing on Mary. She was so small and sweet and delicate, and here we were putting this crazy contraption up to her face and more or less forcing her to stay as still as possible and breathe in the mist. Debby was pretty emotional about having to do this, so I tried to be the voice of reason and assure Debby we were doing the right thing. At this point we were pretty clueless about child care and medicine so I told Debby we had to listen to the doctor. We couldn't just sit around and do nothing while Mary wheezed and choked. Though I felt sorry for Mary and even a little angry at the world for having to use the nebulizer, somehow I felt it was the right thing to do.

After several days, Mary's breathing improved. We were cautioned by the pediatrician that the bronchiolitis may have been deep and severe enough to cause Mary to become asthmatic, so we were to watch for signs of labored breathing in the months and years ahead. It didn't take long for Mary to get sick again, and out came the nebulizer again.

This little scene repeated itself about a dozen times during the first two winters of Mary's life. On most of those occasions she inhaled Albuterol, but there were several times when the cough was persistent and we were prescribed a corticosteroid called Pulmicort to supplement the Albuterol. Corticosteroids are a class of steroid hormones that among other things help in regulation of inflammation.[3] Sure enough, each time we added the corticosteroid, Mary's condition improved much faster than with just the Albuterol alone. Debby cautioned me a few times to go easy on the Pulmicort or avoid it altogether, but Mary's coughing was so frequent that the temptation was great to go for the full blast of Albuterol and Pulmicort to get her back to health as quickly as possible.

While we probably will never know if the extremely frequent Albuterol and/or the Pulmicort treatments contributed in any way to Mary's autism, looking back I regret having used the corticosteroid because I feel it was probably too much medicine for such a small body to handle. While the Pulmicort helped clear Mary's breathing very quickly, a little more patience on my part (to use the Albuterol only perhaps) may have been better for Mary's long-term health. (Though I haven't seen any studies linking corticosteroids to autism, and I'm *not* advancing that argument here, I can't help but think that was a lot of medicine for a little girl and maybe we should have been a little more cautious.)

By the time spring rolled around in each of those first two years, Mary's coughing would subside as the weather warmed up. Mary would go five or six months and not cough at all. During that first summer we took Mary everywhere – to the beach, to the zoo, to the park all the time. It was really a storybook situation and such a happy way to live. She wasn't able to walk yet that first summer – her first steps came at 13 months in October 2002 – but Mary loved to get out of the house and ride along in the stroller.

After another miserable winter of coughing, runny noses and nebulizer treatments, the weather warmed up again and in early June 2003, our son Charlie was born. Mary had a little brother! By then Mary was 20-months old and walking and talking some. She never showed much interest in Charlie though, which was in stark contrast to some of Mary's baby-loving cousins. At that time, Mary had four older cousins living nearby, all within two-and-a-half years of her age. Two of them doted on baby Charlie every opportunity they got. We figured Mary was preoccupied with her own toys and books and didn't have much time for a baby brother. In hindsight, Mary already lacked the social skills and desires to interact with the baby. Though Debby and I were aware that Mary wasn't interacting with the baby much, we never gave it much thought and certainly never considered the idea that our little girl had any kind of developmental issues. In fact, our mindset was quite the opposite.

3. Our Little Genius

We spent the early part of summer in 2003 enjoying our new baby boy and doing all that we could to show Mary how much she was still loved and appreciated, despite the new baby in the house. Near the end of Debby's maternity leave that summer, we took a few days off and drove out on Long Island to the Hamptons for a little family vacation. An infant, Charlie couldn't do much of course but Mary was nearly two-years old and had a great time. By then she would sing to us often and liked nothing more than to sit and look at books. She had mastered the "back-in," her move where she would grab a book, walk over to Mom or Dad, then turn around and back in to one of our laps to have the book read to her. This was an all-day, every-day occurrence.

We all really enjoyed that trip to the Hamptons. We stayed at a small lodge near the ocean and spent a lot of time at the beach. The lodge also had a playground that was perfect for Mary. She ran around the playground singing and laughing. She was as happy as we had ever seen her. Same thing at the beach – our little angel would play in the sand at the edge of the water with so much glee and enthusiasm. Mary's joy was bright and engaging. At night, when we finally had both kids sleeping soundly, Debby and I looked at each other and hugged. It was difficult to put into words how proud we were of our family, how thankful to God we were to have two incredible little bundles of joy. We would stand and watch them sleep for several minutes and just smile at each other.

Before long the vacation was over and it was back to work and reality and day-care. Charlie also started going to the day-care center full-time after 10 weeks. We would drop them both off in the morning around 7:30 a.m. and pick them up at 6 p.m., same as always. Debby and I continued working ambitiously at our jobs, nothing new there. But an interesting thing was happening with Mary, and we started to think we had a little genius on our hands.

Sometime shortly after turning 2, Mary's memory really started to come alive. Her ability to remember stories amazed us. It wasn't just that she could tell you what was going to happen on a given page in one of her books. She could actually recite entire books word-for-word without making any mistakes! Granted, we were still relatively new parents, but we hadn't seen anything like this before. One of Mary's favorite books was "When the Moon is High" by Alice Schertle[4]. It's a hard-cover book with beautiful illustrations by Julia Noonan, and the gist of the story is that a father picks up his baby during the night when the baby can't sleep and the two of them take a stroll outside in the moonlight and see various animals, before the father finally brings the baby back to his crib to fall asleep.

We probably read the book to Mary about 15 times during the month or two after we bought it. She just loved the book. Mary had a pretty typical vocabulary for a two-year old, but to our astonishment, she was memorizing the entire book. Within two months, Mary could actually pick up the book and turn each page, "reading" the text word-for-word as it appeared on the page. Of course she could not really read at that age, but her memory was kicking in and telling her every single word in its correct order on each page! Mary would not only recite the words correctly, but she would enunciate them perfectly and even change the tone and inflection of her voice to match the way it had been read to her. And, to top it off, the text was hardly baby stuff. A sample page has the following text on it:

"Who is humming a lullaby? That's Old Moon up there softly humming, Old Moon on the stars a-strumming sweet dark songs. Now sleep is coming..."

In all, the book has 24 pages of text and illustrations with a total of 342 words. Mary would recite all 342 words in proper order, turning the pages at the proper time, all the while sounding out the words and phrases with the same enthusiasm with which they were read to her originally. It was truly astounding! We had our little genius demonstrate this skill to many of our friends, family and visitors for months. We were so proud of her! What made the whole thing even more enjoyable for us was that it seemed to be bringing such joy to Mary. And, it wasn't just that one book. She recited dozens of books word for word, page by page, without of course being able to read any of the words.

Meanwhile, Mary's day-care teacher began noticing similar advanced skills. I recall one day quite clearly. When I went to pick up Mary, her teacher hurried over to me. The teacher, a large and usually soft-spoken woman, was excited about something. Initially I thought something must be wrong but then the teacher smiled widely.

"Mr. Robertson, you've got to see this," she gushed.

"What is it?" I asked.

"Look what Mary can do!" she said, grabbing a stack of name cards off of her desk.

The teacher proceeded to hold up the name card for each of the children in Mary's class. There were 11 two-year olds along with Mary in that class, and for each child there was a corresponding name card approximately two-inches high by 12-inches long. The children's names were hand written in large block letters on each card.

The teacher held up the first card and asked Mary to whom did the name card belong. Mary "read" the card and immediately gave the correct answer. She did this once again, then again, then again for all 11 cards. She got each one correct, even though she was never asked to memorize those cards and even though at age two she was unable to read. Mary had simply memorized the appearance of each card and had instant memory recall for each card, knowing which letter sequence belonged to each of her classmates.

"She's a genius!" the teacher said. Who were we to disagree?

Mary also demonstrated awareness for her surroundings and picked up on social cues with little trouble. For example, Debby and I attend Catholic Mass every Sunday. One of the traditions at a Catholic Mass is to genuflect before sitting when you arrive at the church. To genuflect is to kneel quickly and make the sign of the cross to oneself just before entering the pew. Not everyone does this anymore, but it's still common to see, and Debby and I usually genuflect when we arrive unless we're overloaded with kids, diaper bags, coats, etc.

When Mary was a little more than 2 years old, we got to mass and started heading toward a pew with open seats. For some reason Mary was first to enter the pew. Without any prompting whatsoever, Mary knelt and genuflected! Debby and I were astounded, and the dozen or so people around us who saw Mary thought it was just the cutest thing they had ever seen. I was quite proud of course. Seeing my daughter in her Sunday best, a pink dress as I recall, genuflecting on her own and entering the pew made me incredibly happy. Clearly this was a blessed child!

4. Mary Peaks At Age 2½

The euphoria over Mary's development was exciting. For months we took great pride in her abilities. We would make a request and Mary would happily oblige us.

"Mary, sing 'Take Me Out to the Ballgame,'" I would say.

"Take me out to the ballgame, take me out to the crowd..." Mary would sing, continuing along with the whole song. All the while she would smile and watch the expressions of joy on my face. She would even punctuate the end of the song by holding up the correct number of fingers for the "It's one, two, three strikes you're out" part of the song, culminating with a backward thumb jab to indicate an umpire's "out" signal. The baseball fan in me was as pleased with Mary as the father in me.

Another of my requests: "Mary, let's say our prayers," I would say.

"Our Father, who art in heaven, hallowed be Thy name," Mary would say, completing the entire Lord's Prayer correctly. She began reciting the prayer precisely, in fact, since just before her second birthday, an amazing ability we thought given the length of some of the words in the prayer.

Mary didn't get sick nearly as often that winter and we were encouraged to say the least. It looked like the day care theory was working after all, and maybe Mary had been exposed to everything already and had built up her immunities. It was Charlie, in fact, who had to use the nebulizer a few times that winter as he went through his first year at day care.

Mary seemed healthy much of the time and was always in such a good mood. She loved to play with her dolls and dollhouse, her play kitchen, and her stacking toys. She also was getting very good at solving puzzles, large wooden puzzles with about 16 pieces. Mary could put a whole puzzle together in a matter of minutes. Somehow she just had an eye for putting them back together. Mary was also good at entertaining herself. She could sit and look through her books for long periods of time. She even started to scribble onto magnetic writing pads that erase with the sliding bar. Though she wasn't drawing pictures or writing her name yet, the fact that she showed interest in writing and holding the stylus pen were encouraging.

But most of all, in the beginning of her third year, Mary loved music. She loved to listen to music, especially anything by Raffi, a Canadian singer who has recorded many classic children's songs over the years. A colleague of mine at work sent us a 3-CD set of Raffi songs and we listened to each and every one of those songs at least a hundred times, to Mary's immense delight. Mary also loved to sing. Her repertoire was extensive, and she performed on command! She would sing "Itsy Bitsy Spider" and make the appropriate hand motions of the spider crawling, rain washing the spider out, etc. She would sing "Twinkle, Twinkle, Little Star" and make a shining diamond hand gesture above her head. She loved songs and she seemed to be picking up on the social interactions involved as she enjoyed the give-and-take of performing for us.

When we got together with Debby's family, there would be as many as five or six young cousins together for hours at a time. Although Mary didn't usually talk much to her cousins, she interacted with them and shared toys with them. She seemed to enjoy family get-togethers and was interested in the same things as her cousins.

Meanwhile at day-care, Mary moved up to the 2-year old room right on schedule with her young peers, many of whom she had been seeing every day for two years. She got along fine with the other kids at day-care and as mentioned earlier, she was somewhat of a darling to the teachers for her sweetness and her emerging abilities.

With Charlie nearing his first birthday and Mary nearing her third birthday, it seemed like the family was in great shape. We were counting our blessings every day and were so pleased with ourselves. At work I co-led a major initiative to develop an off-shore graphic design team in New Delhi, India. I traveled to India to help set up the center, to hire our first on-site leaders, to design the floor layout, etc. It was an enlightening trip for me in many ways, experiencing another culture up close and really expanding my own views of the world. It also proved to be an extremely successful venture for our company, resulting in tremendous annual cost savings. So my job was going well. Debby's position at the bank was mortgage-related, so she was starting to enjoy the early effects of the real estate boom in the United States that lasted another 2-3 years.

We also grew quite comfortable in our home in our little corner of the big city in Whitestone. We enjoyed our grassy backyard and the conveniences of city living without the congestion of Manhattan. Our neighbors across the street had babies the same years we had Mary and Charlie so we had good friends nearby as well. We would go to their house or they would come to ours and the kids played together. We imagined the older kids, both girls, taking dance and gymnastics classes together and having the best of times. Little did we know that within a year our expectations would change so dramatically, that any thought of Mary following along at a dance or gymnastics class would not be realistic. Mary was about to turn inward, shutting out the rest of the world and there was nothing we could do to stop it. In fact, it took us a while to even understand it was happening.

5. The Regression

Looking back I guess there were signs for some time that something wasn't quite right about Mary, but as first-time parents we didn't have anyone with whom we could compare Mary. Sure she didn't interact much with her new brother, but we heard and read a lot about other kids who were the same way. She tended to play by herself at daycare, but with so many toys and things to do there, maybe she was just independent and self-directed. She was a picky eater but many of our friends complained about their kids' eating habits. She had received immunizations according to her pediatrician's recommended schedule, but she never got a shot and that resulted in a high fever or a massive tantrum immediately thereafter, which would have set off alarm bells in our heads.

The bottom line is there just wasn't one dramatic moment when Mary went from acting typical to acting autistic. With Mary, it was like she just slipped away gradually, and after a period of time we could see in hindsight what had happened.

One of the first major red flags with Mary was when, at age 2½, she walked out of the house and headed down the sidewalk on her own. That was a scary one. I had just gotten back from India on a Sunday evening in May 2004. It was my second trip to visit our center there and I had had a wonderful time. Seeing the Taj Mahal up close was an incredible treat. But by the time I had traveled through the night and finally got back home, I was exhausted. My body clock was confused and all I wanted to do was lie on the couch and relax for awhile. Debby put 11-month old Charlie on my chest and I laid on the couch in the living room. Meanwhile, Debby took Mary upstairs and put her to bed, telling Mary she was going to go out and walk the dogs. No sooner did Debby leave then I fell asleep and Mary climbed out of bed. She evidently wanted to follow Mommy and walk the dogs too, because she went right out the side door and down the driveway by herself.

The next thing I knew there was a knock on the front door. Disoriented, I shook the cobwebs from my brain and answered the door. There was our neighbor from three houses down the street with Mary. I was confused to say the least. Our wonderful neighbor, it turns out, had started to drive off somewhere when he noticed Mary walking along the sidewalk by herself, two houses up from ours. He stopped and walked her back to the safety of our home. I was completely embarrassed, first of all, and not really sure what happened.

A few minutes later Debby walked in and asked what the neighbor had wanted. She had seen him leaving when she came around the corner with the dogs. When I told her that Mary had let herself out, Debby burst into tears and asked how we could let that happen. All I could say was that I fell asleep and Mary must have decided to go look for Mommy and the dogs. Though this entire incident took place in less than 10 minutes, it left us shaken for days. The fact that Mary was alone for a few minutes outside in the dark, with a busy cross street further down the block, upset us immensely. We beat ourselves up for being horrible parents, but once again counted our blessings that our neighbor had come along when he did. Of course, Debby probably would have seen Mary within minutes anyway, but who knows what could have happened? We were too busy blaming ourselves to wonder why Mary would venture out of the house alone and head down the street without the slightest fear or worry. Most kids that age would be terrified to go outside alone in the dark and would never consider it, but Mary waltzed right out on her own.

We rationalized that the difficulty getting Mary potty-trained was just bad luck. Everyone we talked to seemed to know of kids who were not potty-trained until age 4 or 5 or even later. That might have been true, but why was it that everyone else in Mary's day-care class figured it out within a few weeks but Mary dragged the process on for months and months and months? Was there any connection to the serious constipation issues she had experienced the previous year? There had been a period of about four months, when Mary was 2, when she would hold her bowel movements as long as possible, sometimes as long as two or three days, then finally cry as she passed a large, hardened stool. The pain of her bowel movements was so great that she would repeat the process over and over to avoid or delay it. For several weeks Mary took a prescription medication to ease her bowel movements, and it did help, so we quickly got her off of the medication and she settled into a normal bowel movement routine. Perhaps that period had traumatized her enough that it affected her desire to become potty-trained. We just didn't know.

This was a critical developmental benchmark that affected her life in day-care, as kids were not allowed to move from the 2-year-old room to the 3-year-old room until they were potty-trained. The infant, 1- and 2-year-old rooms at the day-care center were really more like play areas, but once kids were potty-trained and reached age 3, they moved up to the preschool room. There they began learning to write and sounded out letters and did more sophisticated arts and crafts. It was really more of a school environment in that room than the playtime/babysitting environment of the rooms for younger children.

We watched as Mary's long-time pals one after another figured out the potty training and moved up to the preschool room. But Mary wasn't getting it. We bought books, read internet sites, asked friends and family and sought advice from anyone we saw. And of course we begged and pleaded with Mary. We tried rewarding her with M&Ms or Skittles but had little success. Finally, after about six months, Mary learned to use the potty every time to urinate, but she refused to make poop on the toilet. She would have clean diapers or training pants all day, then all of a sudden we would smell something and sure enough Mary had pooped in her diaper. This went on for a full year.

Finally, somehow, at nearly age 3 ½ Mary got tired of the messes and started using the toilet all the time. There were occasional accidents, and she only wiped about half the time, but she at least she was using the toilet all the time and no longer needed to wear diapers. We were extremely relieved, and at last Mary was allowed to join her friends in the preschool room at day-care. It was winter of 2004-2005, and the cold, dark days outside were a perfect metaphor for the trouble we were having with Mary.

We're not sure exactly when her distaste for interaction kicked in, but by age 3 we noticed that Mary was rarely in the same room with us. We would all be in the family room playing with some toys, then you'd look around and Mary would be gone. She would wander off to the kitchen to play with the refrigerator magnets or head down to the playroom in the basement to use her play kitchen or other toys. Once we'd notice, we'd all head over to wherever Mary was and play along with her. Within a minute, she would head out and find a quiet room somewhere else. It didn't matter what room she went to, as long as she was by herself and didn't have to hear anyone else or interact with anyone.

At first we thought Mary's behavior was almost comical, as if she didn't have the time of day for us! When the behavior continued for several weeks and months, we grew very concerned. To make matters worse, Mary was withdrawing from everything else around her as well. We noticed that the books she used to sit and look at for hours were just sitting in the bookcase unopened unless Charlie pulled them out. She would pick a certain "toy of the day" and become extremely attached to it, unwilling to play with any other toys or games that day. Asking her to do a puzzle with us was pointless, she just ignored the request. Occasionally she would start to make a half-hearted attempt at a puzzle, but within minutes she'd wander off somewhere by herself.

Mary's willingness to try new foods went away completely, and she started begging for the same foods every day; macaroni and cheese, raviolis, chicken nuggets and pizza were among her favorites. She would eat those same foods for every meal of every day if we let her. In fact, she seemed to be craving those foods to the point that if we did not make what she wanted for lunch she would throw a major tantrum.

The tantrum became a regular occurrence, and they were becoming more severe. Whereas she once would just say "OK" if she didn't get her way, now she would throw herself on the floor and scream and cry for several minutes. A tantrum could result from something as simple as not agreeing on what to make for lunch. Every day Mary would walk to the cupboard and take out a box of macaroni and cheese. Quite often we agreed and made it for her, but we had to set limits. We were not going to make it every day!

One day Mary pulled out a box of macaroni and cheese and declared that she wanted it for lunch. When I told her she couldn't have it, she screamed and threw the box across the room.

"I WANT MAC AND CHEESE!" she yelled as loud as she could.

Still I said no, and then she freaked out. Mary flopped to the floor and started writhing around on the tile. She started crying and banging her arms and legs against the floor and against the cupboards. She got completely hysterical and could not calm herself down for several minutes. When I sensed a lull in the storm, I suggested something else she could eat and asked if she wanted a juice box with it. Juice boxes were another highly demanded item, so by offering that and something else for lunch, we got through that tantrum.

It got to the point where she was having full-blown tantrums about once a day. And there would have been many more had we not learned the warning signs and steered clear of tantrum-inciting situations. Periodically we would see Mary become agitated, and she would flap her hands and arms rapidly in front of her as an expression of her irritation or anxiety depending on the situation. Upon seeing this behavior, we would redirect her as quickly as possible to avoid the tantrum.

Perhaps the most puzzling and saddest element of Mary's regression was her unwillingness to speak with anybody, even her Mommy and Daddy. The little girl who the year before would sing "Take Me Out to the Ballgame" when asked no longer sang, not any song, not ever. It was like she completely lost the interest or ability to sing. And I'm telling you, this was a little girl who sang happily half the day during the previous year.

Conversations dried up completely. Not that Mary ever had any in-depth conversations previously, but at least for awhile there was good back and forth thought sharing and play talk. That was quickly fading into history. By age 3 she would only answer questions with a terse "YES" or "NO" and rarely said much else. That doesn't mean that Mary didn't talk; she just didn't talk to anyone else. But her one-sided communication could be quite impressive at times.

Mary was beginning to recite long lines of dialogue from television shows, a behavior we later learned is called *echolalia*. She would sit on the couch with nobody around and recite an entire episode of *Dora the Explorer* dialogue. From what I could tell, she was doing it word for word and even changed the tone of her voice to match the performance she had heard and seen while watching the show previously. It was the same phenomenon she had shown with memorizing books. We tried interrupting this behavior, but once the "tape recorder" in her brain started playing, she had to finish it completely or her world would be out of sync. She would do the same thing with two of her other favorites, *Finding Nemo* and *Sesame Street*.

Something was not right, and we knew we had to do something. So we bought a book on how to communicate with children. Surely we felt that's all it was, just a battle of wills as Mary began exerting her independence. There was no way it could be anything more serious than that. It was a phase that we would work through, and the book had many good ideas for generating interaction and communication. Unfortunately, not a single idea in the book worked. Mary absolutely ignored us all day every day.

We celebrated Christmas in 2004 at Debby's sister Becky's house in a Chicago suburb, and that was too much for Mary to handle. The flight from New York to Chicago went OK, other than Mary's obsession with the tray table in front of her, which she pushed up and pulled down every few minutes to the complete irritation of the man sitting in front of her. At Aunt Becky and Uncle Joe's house, however, the noise and commotion of the holidays in an unfamiliar setting took a toll on Mary. Like many children on the autism spectrum, Mary suffered from sensory overload. She could not tolerate too much noise, so she continually sought isolation and peace in the comfort of the playroom. It was located on the main floor of the house but somewhat away from the noise and congestion of the kitchen/dining room/family room area. There she could escape the chaos and focus on her precious toys.

The most frustrating part of the trip for me was the arrival of Santa Claus on Saturday afternoon and Mary's complete lack of interest. While her other 10 or so cousins laughed and screamed or just looked in awe at the man in the Santa suit, Mary had no interest. In previous years, Mary hadn't seemed aware of Santa either, but she was very young her first two Christmases. The year before, when she was two, Mary didn't have the opportunity to see Santa Claus in person, but we read several books that showed Santa and talked about the night before Christmas and the North Pole and reindeer. So at age three, with Santa in the same room with her, I expected Mary to recognize him and show some enthusiasm.

I vividly remember carrying Mary from the playroom and putting her in the circle of kids around Santa, hoping she would brighten up and realize what was happening right in front of her. Her cousins sat around wide-eyed and took turns saying hi to Santa. Mary didn't care.

"Look Mary, who is that?" I asked.

I wanted Mary to smile and laugh and jump up and down and say "Santa." I really wanted to see that happen and share the moment with her. However, it never happened.

"Mary, who is that guy in the red suit?" I asked again. "Is that Santa? Look Mary, Santa Claus is here!"

I watched in disbelief as Mary got right up and headed straight back to the silence of the playroom without answering me or giving Santa a second look. The incredible opportunity of seeing Santa Claus and receiving some presents from this Christmas icon had no impact on Mary whatsoever.

I followed Mary back to the playroom and asked her to come back out.

"Come on out, Mary," I pleaded once more. "Let's go see Santa Claus!"

"NOOOOOOOOOOOO," Mary shouted loudly. "No Santa."

And that was that. She refused to take even a single picture with Santa either. In fact, she spent most of the rest of the weekend in that playroom and hardly said a word to anyone.

I was more disappointed for myself at that point than for Mary. I was upset that she was cheating me out of such a special father-daughter moment. The opportunity to see Santa and get all excited went by without even the slightest bit of interest from Mary. I felt cheated and disappointed and wondered how the other parents must have felt playing along with the whole Santa charade with their kids. At that point we were still making excuses for Mary, so I told myself that Mary just didn't feel comfortable in a strange house in front of so many people.

While that was probably true, the fact that she didn't muster a hint of enthusiasm for Santa really bothered me.

A few weeks later, in January 2005, my sister Karen was in New York on a business trip and set aside a half day to spend with our family. We had a nice dinner and then spent a few hours in the family room talking while the kids played nearby. Several times we asked Mary a question and were completely ignored. These were not difficult questions or burdensome requests either. The questions were more like "What are you building?" when Mary started stacking some blocks and "Who's your teacher?" when we talked about her new preschool room. Mary was several feet away within clear earshot of our questions and never responded. It was embarrassing, but by that point Debby and I were actually somewhat used to that lack of response. Our expectations were getting lower and lower. We knew Mary's hearing was OK too, because when we got right in her face and asked "Mary, do you want a Popsicle?" she mumbled "Yes" and kept on doing what she was doing. Then, of course, once she finished her treat, she got tired of the inquisition and sought out quiet refuge in another room.

Karen, who's got a daughter of her own, tried to be polite but did address the uncomfortable situation.

"It's surprising that two people as successful as you and Debby would have trouble communicating with Mary," Karen said. "You guys are both so talkative and outgoing. You'd think Mary would be too."

Debby and I squirmed in our seats on the couch.

"We bought a book about communicating with children," I finally said. "Something's not quite right here, but nothing in the book seems to be working so far."

Karen nodded.

"I'm sure you guys will figure it out," Karen replied. "It could be a phase she's going through."

The fact that Karen acknowledged Mary's odd and inappropriate behavior was a red flag to us. Other red flags started coming quickly, and we started to think that maybe we had just been living in denial over Mary's worsening condition the past year.

We were beginning to notice that when we got together with Debby's family, Mary wasn't showing much interest in playing with her cousins anymore. In fact, she hardly spoke to them at all. Clearly she wasn't showing the social awareness and desire for playtime interaction that her cousins of similar ages were showing.

Whenever we got together, Mary would fall into the same routine. Regardless of the time of day or weather, Mary would run to the swing set and spend a good half hour on the swings. Later she would venture into the house and look for the big basket containing plastic figurines of the *Peanuts* gang, Lucy and Charlie Brown being her favorites. At some point Mary would go to the playroom and look for any toys or books related to *Dora the Explorer*. Regardless of who was in the yard or the house or the playroom, Mary did not say hello or even acknowledge them unless she was specifically asked to say hello, and even then she only repeated verbatim the greeting.

Because Mary didn't interact with her cousins anymore, she would wander from one activity to the next and never quite seemed content. She might be playing alongside her cousins one minute then be gone the next. Debby or I were absolutely required to keep an eye on her at all times because we weren't sure when Mary was going to become disinterested in the group and perhaps walk off down the street alone. Every five to ten minutes we'd have to "get a visual" on Mary to make sure she was still in the house or yard, still OK, etc. We often referred to Mary as our "Peach," so the task of making visual contact with Mary on a regular basis became known to Debby and me as "Peach Patrol."

As our stress, tension and disappointment in Mary worsened, our beloved little Charlie was now almost 2 and speaking to us regularly, in stark contrast to his sister almost twice his age. We were hearing things from Charlie already that we were still waiting to hear from Mary. I can still remember our little guy sitting in his car seat, barely age 2, seeing a bus go by and saying "Daddy takes the city bus to work." I almost drove off the road! He not only was correct but he used a complete sentence and did so at the appropriate time since he had just seen a city bus drive past.

In more than three years of driving Mary around town, she had never once commented about anything she saw out the windows. In fact, she had never once even asked where we were going. When it was time to get in the car, Mary put on her coat and off we would go. She showed no curiosity to know if we were driving four minutes to the store or four hours to her see her cousins in upstate New York. We usually talked about where we were going, but if Debby or I did not mention it to Mary, she did not ask. In fact, once Mary started regressing, she went more than a full year without asking a single question! She rarely talked, and when she did it was almost always to express a specific want or need such as for juice or more macaroni and cheese.

As the regression worsened and the darkness took over, we increased our attempts to interact with Mary, speaking to her often, but she just didn't respond. She didn't want to talk to us. She mostly ignored Charlie. She didn't want to eat much. She still had those same beautiful hazel eyes and curly brown hair, but she never looked at us anymore and most of the time she didn't even want to be in the same room with us. Debby and I kept beating ourselves up, questioning ourselves, doubting our parenting skills, crying ourselves to sleep and asking God what was happening to our daughter. Sadly, the bright and happy days of Mary's first two years were getting pushed further and further into the background and fading into memory.

Every so often, though, Mary would curl up in my lap and sit with me. There was still some warmth and affection there, and that meant the world to me. Mary rarely said anything at those times, but she would sit with me for awhile as long as I didn't ask too many questions. I cherished those moments, thanked God for those moments, because they really kept me going. Sadly though, she rarely gave Debby that affection. Though not exactly cold toward her mother, Mary never went out of her way to show much affection either. It was mostly indifference. Even the moments of closeness and affection with me were sporadic. Unfortunately, most of the rest of the time all we knew and saw was a shell of a girl, with little interest in anything other than *Dora, Nemo, Elmo, Peanuts,* swing sets and macaroni and cheese.

6. Our Journey to Recovery Begins

Neither Debby nor I knew much about autism in the early months of 2005, but we were about to get completely immersed in it. In fact, it was already overtaking our lives and would do so more completely in the years to come. We just didn't know it yet.

At 3 years and 3 months, Mary had been promoted to the preschool room at the day-care center, and that meant rejoining her old pals. It also meant getting to know a new teacher, Miss Gina.

Gina was known as the strict teacher at the center, a no-nonsense type who ran a tight ship and was very demanding of the kids and their parents. Gina was a short, stern African-American woman probably in her late-30s at that time. She didn't waste a lot of words and had high expectations of everyone. It didn't take long for Mary to trip up and raise Gina's ire. After about two weeks, when Debby was dropping off Mary one morning, Debby casually asked how things were going.

"Mary doesn't do anything with the class," Gina complained. "She tears up assignments. She only joins the group to eat."

Gina mentioned that Mary often sat on the tables and didn't respond to her instructions or questions. We were still in denial over Mary's condition and were irritated with this new teacher immediately. Surely she just needed to give Mary some time to get used to the new routine.

"She's had two weeks," Gina said. "She can see what she's supposed to do but she doesn't do it. And she doesn't play with any of the other kids either."

Debby and I were annoyed with and saddened by with this report. Up to that time, we had only received positive reports about how bright and wonderful Mary was at school. What happened to the genius who could recite a dozen name cards? Wasn't this the same girl? Now all of a sudden she's a problem kid who doesn't cooperate or interact with others?

Debby and I mulled this over for a few days. We made excuses for Mary. We beat ourselves up some more. But then Charlie would ask a question, make a comment or just do typical kid things, and we knew something was truly wrong with Mary. She was nearly 3½ by this point and needed help.

We spent the next weekend at Debby's sister Rachel's house. Rachel and her husband Tommy are Mary's godparents, and they had watched her grow and develop. Debby and Rachel spent a long time that weekend discussing Mary's behavior, both at home and in the new preschool room at day-care. Rachel asked if we ever considered the idea of having Mary tested for a learning disability.

"It couldn't hurt," Rachel said. "Maybe it's nothing. But at least you'll know. And if it's something, then you can get help."

The nudge from Rachel was exactly what we needed, even if we didn't really want to hear it. Looking back, we give Rachel a lot of credit for giving that advice. It probably wasn't easy to suggest that our child had problems severe enough to warrant a professional evaluation. No parent really wants to hear that. The advice also suggested that Mary wasn't developing correctly, an opinion that we could have easily perceived as a knock on our parenting capabilities. Of course that's not what Rachel was saying. She took a risk suggesting an evaluation, knowing that her well-intended comments could have led to an argument or created tension among us. However, we were concerned enough about Mary's behavior to listen to Rachel's advice, and we accepted the nudge in the spirit with which it was given.

The next day we made an appointment with Mary's pediatrician and within a week we were all sitting in his office. The doctor we met with had seen Mary many times during the previous three years and was aware of her medical history. As we talked about Mary's behavior, the doctor watched Mary. He asked her a few questions and got no response. She never made eye contact, instead mostly sat on my lap and looked around the room.

The doctor ran his fingers through his graying hair and first commented that Mary was a very affectionate, beautiful young girl. We smiled and nodded. He talked about a wide variety of behavior disorders and said we should pursue testing. We stopped smiling and grew anxious. Finally, he said the words you can never quite prepare yourself to hear.

"She may be on the autism spectrum," the doctor said. "She's not making eye contact. But she is high-functioning and affectionate so it may be a mild case."

And with that the doctor gave us a plain piece of paper with two names and phone numbers on it: one was the pediatric neurologist who could give us a medical evaluation of Mary's condition, and the other was the name of the woman in the New York City School District special education office who handles preschool-age testing and evaluations. We thanked the doctor and quickly headed outside.

When we stepped outside the door, the whole world had changed. Everything looked and felt different than it had a half hour earlier. The clouds were a little darker and the sky much grayer. All the sunlight had vanished. People walked by on the sidewalk in front of us, oblivious to the gloom and despair welling up within Debby and me. A bus pulled up on the corner ahead; some people got off, a few people got on and away went the bus. I remember thinking how strange it was that all of those people were going about their business as if this was just another day in the life, yet here we were having our entire world turned upside down and torn apart. Why wasn't everyone stopping and acknowledging our horror?

I felt tears welling up in my eyes but I knew I had to be strong. It was too soon to leap to any conclusions. This preliminary diagnosis hurt, but in-depth testing would be much more definitive, and until those tests were done there was no need to panic. Maybe the doctor was giving us a worst-case scenario and in reality, Mary would be just fine. Then I looked over at Debby and she had tears running down her face.

"He said 'autism,'" Debby said. Her tears flowed freely. She was right and I knew it. It was time to stop the denial, stop the excuses, stop beating ourselves up and stop hoping for instant miracles. This wasn't a phase that would just go away. We were staring straight into the face of autism.

It was early February and it was cold outside. It was getting darker and nobody was walking up to us to give us the answers we needed. We knew we were on our own. As we hugged and cried outside the doctor's office we had no idea what was going to happen next. We had the sledgehammer diagnosis of autism to deal with, and only a piece of paper with a couple of names and phone numbers to get us started. We were pretty clueless about autism and special education in general, but we knew that Mary needed us more than ever. We were determined to fight to save our little girl from slipping further away.

We called the NYC School District office the next day and made an evaluation appointment for Mary, then spent the next few weeks reading books, magazines and hundreds of online articles about autism. It was all autism, all the time for Debby and me. We were determined to be as educated about this new foe as possible. We were saddened to learn that the autism diagnosis rates were rising, and further saddened to learn that no cure existed. We were encouraged that research was increasing and that several large organizations had formed to raise autism awareness and generate funding for research.

We were also amazed to learn how very differently each case of autism manifested itself. Some kids on the higher functioning side of the spectrum were verbal and outgoing but had some quirkiness to them, such as an extreme interest in a subject like trains or maps. These kids were often otherwise "typical" and attended regular public education classes. Kids at the other end of the spectrum had sensory issues, including aversions to light, noise, crowds or certain textures or smells, and sometimes all of the above. Other kids didn't talk at all, even into their teenage years. Some kids were potty-trained at the typical age; others never could master toilet skills. Some children were very cold and distant from everyone, including family members, while others were warm and pleasant but affected in other ways.

The autism spectrum, we quickly realized, was truly wide and encompassed a great variety of symptoms. And in each case there were mothers and fathers and brothers and sisters and extended family members and therapists dealing with the heartaches, the tantrums, the quirks, the silence and just the grind of getting through another day.

It seemed like every time Debby or I were feeling sorry for ourselves, we read about another family dealing with more challenges than we were. While we certainly didn't take any joy in that, we began to realize that Mary did have some skills and abilities to build upon, and we began focusing on giving thanks for her strengths instead of just pitying ourselves and dwelling on her shortcomings.

One book that proved especially helpful in those early days was *Overcoming Autism: Finding the Answers, Strategies and Hope that can Transform a Child's Life*, by Lynn Kern Koegel and Claire LaZebnik. [5] I loved the title immediately. I hadn't thought of overcoming autism before, because we had read that there was no cure for it. However, the book took a positive and proactive approach to the disorder, focusing on how early and well-planned interventions can lead to breakthroughs that reduce the symptoms of autism. Maybe it couldn't be cured, but autism could be *overcome!* I think I read the book in two days and passed it on to Debby who also read it with great interest. The book changed our outlook considerably. Instead of predicting doom and gloom for Mary, we began to focus on getting her the help she desperately needed.

7. Evaluating Mary

The New York City School District serves 1.1 million children according to its website, a daunting challenge that has left the school system with its fair share of critics and fans. The city is enormous, with 8.2 million people in the five boroughs of New York City in 2006 according to the U.S. Census Bureau, including 2.2 million in Queens County. All those New Yorkers are diverse, with a tremendous immigrant population that doesn't always speak much English. In fact, according to the U.S. Census Bureau, 53% of Queens households speak a language other than English in the home.

This of course means that in every pocket of the city there are lots and lots of children who go home every day to parents or other family members who speak a language other than the English spoken at school all day long. It must be an incredible challenge to educate such a diverse population! We knew going in that the school system would be big, challenging and bureaucratic. We could only hope its special education department would be organized and well run.

Many of the diverse and wonderful children in Queens have terrific talents and abilities. They assimilate quickly into their schools, make friends and succeed. They are often great role models for other students and parents alike. There are hundreds of inspired and talented teachers educating the students. The huge number of students also means there are plenty of children with special needs.

We had heard friends and neighbors talk about the NYC school system, somewhat jokingly, saying that the top 10% are given great opportunities and the 10% with special needs get great care, but everyone in the middle gets pushed along like cattle. The general perception of NYC schools back in 2005, from people we talked to, was that the educational experience would vary drastically by the luck of location, teacher and parental involvement. Such is probably true of any school district, but with the huge number of students processing through New York City each year, the challenges in our district had to be compounded.

Nevertheless, we needed help and we needed the school district to help us. Our little girl needed an evaluation, and this was going to be the next step in our journey. Mary was nearly 3½, and everything we read online said early intervention was the key to success. We probably should have started the evaluation process nine months earlier, when Mary first started regressing, but it had taken awhile to understand the scope of Mary's issues. Fortunately Mary still had a year and a half to go before Kindergarten, so we had some time on our side.

The day after meeting with our pediatrician, I called the NYC school district representative for preschool special education in our region. She was supportive and understanding. Though we still had much to learn about autism and had many fears and questions, at least we weren't alone anymore! Our NYC preschool representative was no longer just a name on a piece of paper but a real person who would help start us on the path to, well, something. We weren't sure yet where the path was going but we knew we were getting started. The woman said she would send us a list of locations where we could get Mary's behavior evaluated, and she specifically recommended the Whitestone School for Child Development.

This was to be the first of many signs that something spiritual and bigger than us was taking place, because when the list of testing sites came in the mail a few days later, I saw dozens of choices. But one place jumped off the page; the address for the Whitestone School for Child Development was the very same address as our church, Holy Trinity Roman Catholic Church.

We had been members of the Holy Trinity parish for five years at that point, and we knew the church had a private elementary school, but neither Debby nor I had any idea that the church subleased a portion of its school building to a small special education group called The Whitestone School for Child Development. The location was surely a sign from above that we finally were heading in the right direction. Mary had been baptized in 2001 in the main church, just steps away from the school. Debby and I had both sung in the church choir for two years prior to Mary's birth, and the choir had organized a baby shower for us the summer before Mary was born. We felt warmth, love and community in our parish, and now we were taking one of the first major steps in our journey right there in the parish school building! Needless to say, we quickly called the Whitestone School and set up an appointment for Mary's testing.

While we waited for the behavioral testing date to arrive, we took Mary to see the neurologist for a medical evaluation. We had no idea what the neurologist was going to do, but our pediatrician recommended that we see a neurologist, so we did. The meeting with the neurologist ended up being quite brief. In fact the meeting was so brief that when Debby arrived 15 minutes late she missed the whole visit!

In the 12-minute meeting, the neurologist measured Mary's head and felt her stomach. He looked at her neck, tongue, shoulders and posture. He took notes. He listened as she echoed dialogue from television shows and he saw that she rarely made eye contact. He asked Mary some questions, which she did not answer. He asked me some questions about Mary, particularly her willingness to socialize with other children. I told the doctor that she rarely socialized anymore and did not have any peer friends.

That was pretty much it, 12 minutes and we were out of there. The doctor wrote up an evaluation and basically said that Mary appeared to be physically sound and in good general health, but she lacked appropriate language skills and made little eye contact. He concluded that "based on these findings, I believe Mary may have a pervasive developmental disorder and she may actually fall within the realm of an autistic spectrum disorder. I therefore suggest she undergo a thorough pediatric neuropsychological evaluation."

The neurologist's initial report pretty much confirmed our growing suspicions. We nevertheless held out a sliver of hope that the testing at the Whitestone School would somehow reveal something different. These tests were scheduled in late February and completed over parts of two or three days. We brought Mary to the school and they asked if Mary could be bribed with treats to cooperate. They had Froot Loops on hand and those proved to be quite helpful. The evaluators used the Froot Loops as rewards for Mary's participation… answer a question and get a treat.

During the testing, Mary was asked to put together wooden puzzles, to work with blocks, to play with toys, etc. Periodically the evaluator would ask Mary questions and/or play along with her. We were told that Mary rarely answered the questions, never made eye contact and preferred parallel play over interactive play with the evaluator. Her attention span was short and, unless Mary was offered a treat, she rarely acknowledged the evaluator. When rewarded, Mary did identify most letters and numbers and she was able to answer some basic questions. The tests clearly indicated that Mary's development was about a year behind schedule at that point – she was said to be 33% delayed in her language skills and lacked social interaction skills. The evaluators were very thorough, even going so far as to make a visit to Mary's day care center. There they watched her behavior and lack of interaction with peers, confirming their test results.

Concerned parents should talk to their pediatricians and push to have their children evaluated as soon as there is any doubt about the child's development. It is critical to act early because if the child does have autism, the sooner the treatments start the better chance the child has for making substantial progress.

The evaluators from the Whitestone told us they believed Mary definitely had at least some level of autism. She was a kid "on the spectrum" and in need of early intervention. The testing at the Whitestone School revealed that Mary's receptive language skills and expressive language skills were both found to be at a 2-year-old level, a 33% delay. Interestingly, the evaluators determined that Mary's IQ was in the normal range, so we saw that as reason for optimism. Mary had intelligence; it just wasn't manifesting itself properly at that time.

The Whitestone School representatives were sincere and wonderful and they sent their report to our school district representative confirming Mary's need for services. They suggested that she be placed in a small class so Mary would not have distractions and could receive more personal attention from the teacher than she would get in a larger class. However, they also pointed out that their own Whitestone School was operating at full capacity, and with the school year nearly over we would have to find another location for Mary's schooling to begin.

At that time Mary was still attending the day-care facility full-time, and Gina was warming up to Mary. We kept Gina informed of the evaluations, to a degree, and she told us that her own son had been tested for a learning disorder within the NYC School District a few years before. Gina, with a new perspective on Mary's behavior, took it upon herself to include Mary in activities as much as possible and reached out to her more often, rather than letting her drift off alone.

Noting Mary's sensory issues, especially an aversion to hair brushing, Gina began putting a "scrunchie" ribbon in Mary's hair each morning. At first Mary would pull it right out, but eventually she warmed up to Gina as well and let Gina put the scrunchie in her hair. This went on for several weeks, to the point that after awhile, Mary would leave the scrunchie in her hair for as long as 15-20 minutes!

Nevertheless, we knew Mary's days at day-care were numbered. While we waited for the NYC school district to process Mary's evaluation, we could only wonder where the journey would take us next. Debby and I prayed that we would choose the right school and setting for Mary. We didn't want her to travel too far for preschool and we hoped the environment would be warm and welcoming.

Before we got too far into our search, we got a call out of the blue from The Whitestone School. One of the children in an 8-1-2 class was leaving the school, creating an opening for Mary. Divine intervention was at work again! An 8-1-2 class, we would soon find out, was a class with no more than 8 students, at least 1 teacher and 2 teaching assistants. This was exactly what Mary needed! We were thrilled and amazed at our good fortune. Mary would be able to attend school right there by our church, only a mile from our house. And, she would be learning in a small class setting with a special education teacher and two assistants. We could not have been more thrilled. It was early April by this point, and we were told that Mary could join the school effective May 1, 2005. And that's exactly what she did.

After more than three years of full-time day-care, Mary was about to embark on a new path. We were sad to say goodbye to the other children and parents at the day-care center, many of whom we had seen nearly every day for three years. We were also sad to be saying goodbye to the "normal" world, the world where kids grow up and play together and listen to their teachers. But that was not to be Mary's calling, and we knew that. I was never personally embarrassed about Mary's diagnosis, just determined to do everything possible to see her improve. Moving on from day-care was the next step in that direction. Of course, Charlie would still attend the day-care center for another year until he was old enough for preschool, so in reality we weren't really saying goodbye for good. Nevertheless, Mary's current and former teachers made her a nice going-away scrapbook and wished her well.

8. Part-Time for Dad

The ripple effect of Mary's diagnosis was dramatic. She would no longer be dropped off at day-care at 7:30 a.m. and left to play there all day until 6 p.m. Going forward she would start school at 8 a.m. and get home at 2 p.m. Debby and I were both still working full-time and enjoying our jobs, despite the stress of dealing with Mary's deteriorating skills and the increasing demands of the school district. With all the testing, meetings and appointments, keeping any kind of work schedule was getting difficult.

Debby and I discussed our work situation and spent hours mulling over the possibilities. While I was earning a good living and enjoyed my work, it was quickly losing importance for me given Mary's challenges. Debby was doing well enough in sales for us to manage on one income, so we decided that the best thing for our family was for me to quit my job and focus on the kids, primarily on Mary's behavior but also very much on Charlie as well.

Truthfully, we had been considering this idea for quite awhile. As far back as Mary's third birthday in September of 2004, six months before her diagnosis, Debby and I had talked about Mary's troubling behavior and discussed our options. We had talked about the long hours that Mary spent in day-care and whether that was impacting her behavior. At that point I had begun to consider cutting back at work or quitting altogether, but it had been all talk and no action. Once we had Mary's diagnosis and a placement for her in the Whitestone School, it was time for me to take that action.

As much as I knew cutting back at work would be necessary, I knew my manhood was at stake and I wasn't quite ready to be Mr. Mom, a stay-at-home Dad. While I was reading more and more stories about guys who were leaving their jobs to stay home with the kids while Mom worked, I felt that there was still a certain stigma to that arrangement. No matter how practical and correct the decision to quit and stay at home might be, for too long I had been worried that I would be seen by friends, neighbors and acquaintances as less significant in some way. Any time a guy is out and meets people for the first time, whether at a party or family function or even just the barber shop, inevitably somebody will ask, "What do you do?" I wasn't sure I was ready to say, "I stay at home with the kids," even though I knew darn well that that job was more demanding and exhausting, and in many ways more important than any other job.

While gender roles are changing in this country, the fact is that hundreds of years of defined roles for men and women are ingrained in our national psyche. So just as many mothers who work outside the home deal with second-guessing and self-doubt about their jobs at times, the same is true for many stay-at-home men. We face our own second-guessing and doubts about staying home with the kids instead of getting out there and bringing home the bacon. Self-doubts or not, the time had finally come to move forward on this decision. I convinced myself that I had to quit working. It was the right thing to do for my family so I would do it.

It was about this time that God stepped in again and made everything work out OK for us. It's amazing how often that happens. I prayed that I was making the right decision to quit working, and then I made up my mind to do it. My boss, Marlene, was based in Chicago, so I would have to quit over the phone. It wasn't an ideal way to resign, but it was better than sending her an email. So with much nervousness and a little uncertainty, I called Marlene.

"Marlene, I have some bad news," I said. "Mary has been diagnosed with autism. We knew for awhile that something was wrong with her because she hasn't been talking to us much. In fact basically she has been avoiding people for the past year."

"I'm sorry to hear about that," Marlene said.

"Thanks, we're still coming to grips with the diagnosis," I said. "But already it's pretty clear that it's going to be a big time commitment to care for Mary now. We can't just leave her at day-care anymore."

I explained to Marlene that Mary would have a new school schedule and how someone had to be home at 2 p.m. to watch her for the rest of the day. I let her know there would be meetings and doctor visits related to Mary's autism. Then I told Marlene how Debby and I had talked about this at great length and that even though I was enjoying the challenges of my job and felt I was still doing a great job, my family came first.

"I'm going to have to resign," I told Marlene. "I still love my job but for Mary's sake, I think this is something I have to do."

A sense of relief came over me after I said those words, as I had been dreading the conversation for days. But I also felt saddened that I would be leaving behind my professional identity and a job that I was doing well.

Marlene was quiet for what seemed like a minute but was probably only a few seconds. I will be forever grateful to Marlene for her response.

"I understand what you're saying," Marlene said. "But before you resign, let's think this over. Once you quit, it's very difficult to return if you change your mind, with budgets and approvals and all that stuff. Perhaps you'd be better off taking a leave of absence while you see how things go. Or, since you mentioned that Mary will be going to school all morning, would you consider working part-time while she's at school?"

I was stunned. I originally had thought that a part-time arrangement would be a great way to stay connected to work and the "grown up" world, but given my global responsibilities and Marlene's strong work ethic, I was sure that she would never even consider such a thing. However, not only did Marlene consider it do-able, she's the one who suggested it as an option! Needless to say I quickly accepted her generous offer.

So in early 2005, I switched to a 20-hour work week, with most of my work being done in my home office. I would commute to midtown Manhattan only a few days each month going forward, so that I would be home most days to watch Mary and Charlie after preschool let out. Working primarily from home would allow me to schedule meetings and appointments during the day, then make up those hours later in the afternoon or night as needed. And though my salary was sliced in half, I was still bringing in some decent income and taking a little of the bread-winner pressure off Debby.

With Marlene on board, I just had to inform my global colleagues of my decision. Again, I wasn't sure what kind of reaction I would get. I suspected there might be some jealousy of my working-from-home arrangement, as well as some scrutiny as to how well I would be able to do my job while working just 20 hours per week. I knew though, as did Marlene, that I would do everything I could to make the transition seamless and keep the department running efficiently. There were a few administrative tasks that I would be delegating, but otherwise I was still going to be running the department.

So it was with some hesitation and nervousness that I typed out an email and sent it to my global reports. My colleagues were not told of Mary's diagnosis, only that I needed to cut back on my hours for family reasons and that I was still going to be running the department. I clicked the SEND button then held my breath and waited for the responses to come in. To my surprise and delight, I received about a dozen encouraging emails. Having the support of my colleagues really helped, and I never looked back. I also never forgot the wisdom, compassion and generosity of my boss Marlene, who could have just let me quit and walk away. Instead she helped keep me focused and connected and involved, all the while I was still available to address Mary's growing needs.

9. Bottoming Out

W e anxiously awaited Mary's first day at the Whitestone School. To be honest, it couldn't come soon enough. Mary's behavior had deteriorated to the point that we were afraid we were losing her completely. By Spring 2005, Mary was just past age 3½ and had retreated almost completely into her own little world. Her vocabulary was strong and growing, but she used it exclusively for echolalia, repeating lines and lines of *Dora the Explorer, Finding Nemo, Blues Clues* and *Peanuts* television programs all day long. Asking her questions became pointless because she ignored all inquiries.

Besides the social withdrawal and the echolalia, Mary started showing more troubling behavior. At times she would put her fingers in front of her face, just inches from her nose, and wiggle her fingers around. She acted out imaginary scenes with her hands, using her fingers as puppets. Sometimes she would verbalize an imaginary conversation between her left hand and her right hand, other times she would just screech and mutter as she worked her hand puppets in front of her face. This behavior could last anywhere from 10 seconds to three or four minutes, depending on how much dialogue she was imagining.

Mary started waking up at least once or twice a week in the middle of the night. And once she was awake, there was no telling how long she would stay up. It was common for her to wake up at 2 a.m. and stay awake until 4 or 5 a.m. The whole time she would be talking to herself, reciting lines of dialogue and giggling. And it's not like Debby and I let Mary watch television all day, building up her repertoire. We both strived to limit our children's television to one hour per day, with some days more successful than others. Nevertheless, Mary's internal tape recorder captured every line of dialogue she heard and at night the playback kicked in. If she woke up, the recorder in her head turned on and no matter how tired she was, she would lay in her bed and continue to recite dialogue. Most people would assume that such behavior from an exhausted 3-year old would taper off after 10 or 15 minutes, but Mary would literally lay in bed and recite dialogue for as long as two hours, in the middle of the night.

These night wakings were a huge detriment to the rest of the family. Charlie often slept through them, amazingly, but I could not. A light sleeper, I would be awakened at the first peep Mary made and would often be awake for the next two hours. Debby usually woke up as well. No matter what we said or asked of Mary, no matter how we pleaded, she would not or could not go back to sleep. Sometimes she would finally fall asleep by 4 or 5 a.m., other times she never went back to sleep. The next day, Debby and I often went to work exhausted and sleep deprived. We had slept more when Mary was an infant than we did at that point!

We knew that Mary's diet was a mess and getting worse, although we didn't think at the time that there was any correlation between her night wakings and her diet. As mentioned earlier, Mary ate chicken nuggets, macaroni and cheese, pizza and pasta for almost every meal. Healthier foods such as carrots, apples, watermelon, bananas and grilled chicken, all of which she ate regularly as a 2-year old, would get pushed around her plate but never put in her mouth.

Fortunately, Mary got plenty of exercise, albeit on her own terms. We enrolled her in a local gymnastics program when she was 2 and she stayed in the program for two years. The second year she and Charlie attended together, and the program was set up so that a parent accompanied each child throughout the class. It was an ideal situation for Mary, because she could run around and jump on the trampoline and crawl through padded tunnels for an hour each Saturday. Part of the program was supposed to be kids listening to the instructor and following a few basic routines each week. Mary thrived on the routine parts of the class; however, she had no ability to focus and stay on task during the instructional part of the class. Rather than pay attention to the instructor, Mary would run off to the trampoline or the rope swing while most of the other kids stayed seated. It was all we could do to restrain her and keep her with the group. This went on week after week, month after month.

(At age 4 Mary "aged out" of the parent-student class and had to attend on her own, while Debby and I stayed off the gym floor in the parents' waiting area. At the first trial class, we left after 10 minutes knowing it would not work. Mary thought it was play time and didn't pay attention to the instructors. Though the gymnastics folks were wonderful and gave Mary plenty of opportunities, they had to maintain some order for the class to enable the other students to learn. So regrettably, Mary was not allowed to participate in her weekly gymnastics classes any more, which seemed to bother Debby and me more than Mary.)

In addition to gymnastics, Mary and Charlie spent two years in a structured swim program in nearby Forest Hills. Because the pool was indoors, we were able to send the kids to swimming lessons year-round for two full years without interruption. The classes were set up so that for the first three-month session, the parent stayed in the water with the child. Then for the second three-months the child swam with an instructor, without the parent in the water. Usually when the parent got out of the water there was one instructor working with two small children. With older children, the ratio increased to 3 or 4 students per instructor. That was the exact path that Charlie took, but Mary was not able to follow along. In fact, the swim program made an exception for us and allowed me to stay in the water with Mary for almost two years!

Once Charlie started swimming with an instructor, Mary and I followed along. Whatever the instructor had Charlie do, I had Mary do the same thing. For some reason, unlike almost every situation at home, Mary listened and followed along with whatever I asked her to do in the water. She initially needed me for safety reasons, but even as her swimming abilities improved she continued to listen to me and to follow along. By the end of the second year I was ready to get out of the pool and have Mary and Charlie work with instructors. Sounded great, but it didn't work. Mary would not follow the instructors. As soon as the instructor looked away or started working with Charlie, Mary swam off on her own. This continued with several instructors until she was paired up with Leah.

Leah was different from the other swim instructors. She was demanding and her temperament was a bit rough around the edges. But she took a quick liking to Mary and the two of them spent four months working together in the pool. Leah, a muscular Caucasian woman with long brown hair, appeared to be in her early 20s. She saw Mary as a challenge. When Mary started to swim away, Leah shook her head and smiled then quickly grabbed Mary's ankle and lightly yanked her back. It wasn't a mean-spirited or punishing yank, just a where-do-you-think-you're-going-yank to remind Mary who was in charge.

Before long, Leah had Mary swimming from one end of the pool to the other, lengthwise, correctly using a kickboard and even properly diving into the pool. None of this had happened with the other instructors; most were too nice and let Mary take advantage of them (or in some cases, couldn't possibly keep up with Mary while helping another child.).

Unfortunately, Leah left the program when the spring instruction period ended. We gave it another try with a pleasant young female instructor during the summer session, but she was too nice and Mary just didn't work well with her. Mary swam away on her own every chance she got and rarely cooperated. Her skills were good enough to allow her to move safely around in the pool, but she needed more discipline in her strokes and technique. She was not interested in cooperating and improving, she just saw the swimming lessons as play time. When it got to the point that lessons had become a waste of time, we had to stop going there too. What was once a bright spot for Mary, her willingness to cooperate with Leah and make progress swimming, was gone.

Besides her inability to follow instructions from her recreational teachers, we knew that Mary was falling behind academically. Other kids in the neighborhood, her day-care classmates and cousins her age were starting to write letters and numbers and some were writing their names. A few were even sounding out letters. A neighbor girl across the street close to Mary's age was already writing her name and creating fancy arts and crafts at her preschool. Meanwhile, Mary could barely hold a pencil, could not write letters and in fact could not even draw a straight line. If given paper and a pencil or pen, Mary scribbled a little bit and that was it. She had no interest in writing or listening to instructions. We often tried to explain how to write something but Mary quickly tuned us out.

I remember feeling jealous and embarrassed when I saw the neighbor's arts and crafts taped to the front of their refrigerator. Their daughter not only completed the project but had written her own name on the bottom of the paper. I really don't remember exactly what the project was, but I do remember seeing her name clearly written at the bottom in a child's handwriting. I was starting to wonder if Mary would ever be able to write her own name or complete a class assignment. I really didn't know, because we just weren't connecting with Mary.

Something as simple as a neighbor's arts and crafts project can push you into an unexpected emotional low. I remember overreacting inwardly when I saw how much our neighbor could do by age 3 while Mary wasn't even close. I thought to myself that here I was, a long-time honors student married to an honors student, both of us college graduates, and yet our daughter couldn't write her name. What kind of future could she possibly have, if she already was falling behind in such simple things as writing her name? Would Mary ever catch up? Would she go on to high school and college, or would she stay withdrawn into her world and never amount to anything? Would she ever have the focus and initiative to complete a school project, or would she spend the rest of her life watching *Dora the Explorer* and *Sesame Street* videos? Truthfully I didn't know, and I was allowing a seed of pessimistic doubt to creep in.

You allow yourself a few moments of pity and then you have to quickly move on though, which is what I did. That's what Debby and I did. We were determined that Mary would be successful, and we focused on the fact that she was starting at a new school and would be getting more help soon.

So even though we felt ourselves at rock bottom, we were extremely hopeful that the professionals at the Whitestone School could get through to Mary and get her basic academic skills up to speed in time for Kindergarten. Surely they would have some great techniques that would turn Mary around. And they did, but the turnaround didn't happen overnight.

10. The Mighty IEP

As per the Individuals with Disabilities Education Act (IDEA),[6] all students across America who receive special education services are required by federal law to have an annual Individual Education Program (IEP). The IEP is very detailed and should be taken very seriously by everyone who participates in the IEP discussions. The IEP is a document that lists upcoming goals and objectives for the student. It also contains the list of special services the child will receive from the school district, and the amount of those services that will be mandated. These services often include transportation to and from school, speech therapy, physical therapy, occupational therapy, a small class size, etc. The IEP also may contain information about special accommodations that may be made for the child, such as being permitted to take tests one-on-one with a teacher.

It's especially critical for parents to speak up during the IEP process and aim high: negotiate for the most services possible and at the highest occurrences. Parents can always work backward during the process and make concessions, but they should start out by demanding as much or more care that they think their child needs. Special services can be expensive, so school district representatives may be inclined to downplay or put limits on the frequency of services provided. Parents are the child's greatest advocate, though, and it's during the IEP process that they need to speak out and stand firm if they believe certain services are necessary. For example, don't settle for speech therapy twice a week for 15 minutes if you think your child needs speech therapy five times a week for a half hour per day. Demand the most and compromise only if you must.

The week before Mary started at the Whitestone School, we returned to the NYC Special Education office in Queens for Mary's first IEP meeting. We met with our preschool representative from the school district and with Mary's new teacher, Miss D from the Whitestone School. We were very naïve as to the whole IEP process and were unaware of some of the horror stories we heard later (people have had to bring lawyers to IEP meetings to fight for various needed services.) In hindsight, we were treated very fairly and Mary was provided with a good foundation to begin her special education.

During the first IEP meeting, parents are somewhat at the mercy of the school system because they don't always know what services are available, how many hours of speech or occupational therapy other kids are getting, etc. Prior to their IEP meeting, parents are advised to ask other parents at the school what types of services their children are receiving, how many hours of therapy each week, etc. This would be very helpful in getting the first IEP started correctly. Otherwise, the process usually unfolds with the school administrator reviewing the child's diagnosis and tests and then suggesting some kind of plan containing related services that may or may not be adequate. The better prepared the parent is before the first meeting, the better chance the parent has of swaying the administrator toward more realistic levels of services. (IEPs can be modified later and updated with increased levels of services if the child is not responding well or showing improvement in school. But that can take months or even a full year to get into the IEP depending on the awareness of teachers and parents and the availability of school administrators.)

Mary's first IEP, dated April 20, 2005, specified that she would be placed in a special education preschool environment not to exceed 8 students, with a minimum of 1 teacher and 2 teaching assistants. The IEP stated that Mary was to receive 5 days of special education each week, with 5 hours of services each day. It also stated that Mary was required to receive two, 30-minute sessions of speech therapy each week and two, 30-minute sessions of occupational therapy each week. Her IEP stated her age as 3 years and 7 months – still young enough that many people would consider her schooling as early intervention but ideally, we could have started sooner. One thing her IEP did not mention anywhere was the word "autism." At that point, Mary's behavior and skills were labeled as "delayed" throughout. Considering that Mary had spent the previous years hanging out in the periphery of day-care, avoiding interaction and receiving little social interaction, we were thrilled to have the IEP in hand. It was physical representation of the start of Mary's long road back.

One thing I had read about in the *Overcoming Autism* book was the need to assemble a team of people to help your child. When I first read that guidance I remember being somewhat overwhelmed at the thought of having to put together such a team. However, going through the NYC School District's processes, jumping through the many hoops to get Mary placed at the Whitestone School, we were being handed a team of helpers for Mary. She soon had a teacher, two assistant teachers, a speech therapist, an occupational therapist, a social worker and a school psychologist working with her every week. The school district was doing an excellent job for us.

As it turned out, we were extremely fortunate to land that spot in the Whitestone School. Besides the close proximity of the school to our house and the connection to our Catholic church, the school was well-run by some great people. The special services stipulated in Mary's IEP were followed very closely and she received a tremendous amount of speech and occupational therapy along with her intensive class work. As Mary grew and we moved on to other schools in the years that would follow, we heard stories about other students never seeing anything close to the services stipulated on their IEPs, either through lack of resources at various schools or lack of oversight by school officials. Sometimes, believe it or not, IEPs are not followed closely because parents just don't get involved or ask questions about how closely the services are being followed.

In addition to stipulating required services, the IEP defines annual goals and short-term objectives for the student. The goals are then measured quarterly, each time with a look back at how much progress the student has made and a look forward at whether the evaluator expects the student to meet the goal that year. Mary's first goals were:

1. To improve play skills during structured play periods
2. To improve peer play and socialization skills
3. To develop and improve comparison skills (e.g. big/little)
4. To develop and improve personal responsibility in the classroom setting
5. To improve ability to remain on task
6. To increase interactions with peers and adults
7. To develop and improve pre-readiness skills during structured activities
8. To improve understanding of quantitative concepts (e.g., counting, more/less)

Each of these goals had four to five short-term objectives attached to them. In total, Mary had about 35 short-term objectives written out in her IEP, each with the intention of improving her various skill sets in order to prepare her for Kindergarten and to increase her interaction with other students. The speech and occupational therapists at the Whitestone School also added their own sets of goals and objectives, bringing into clarity about 50 short-term objectives for Mary. We had assembled our team around Mary, and now it was time to turn them loose on her and see what miracles they had up their sleeves.

11. Hello, Special Education

W hile filling out the paperwork for Mary's enrollment at the Whitestone School, we were encouraged to send in a request for busing. Debby and I rolled our eyes and practically laughed at each other. Put Mary on the bus, at age 3½, when we live so close to the school? What an absurd idea! We could drive there faster, and besides Mary was still so small and young to be put on a bus and be taken away each day. Nevertheless, we were persuaded to do so because the administrators felt that the kids coped better with the new school when they had time on the bus to think about where they were going and to get prepared for the day ahead. It was a transition between home and school, and the folks at the Whitestone School were sure that the kids performed better that way. When we saw they were serious we agreed to try it for one week.

We bought Mary a backpack (*Dora* theme, of course) and started talking to her about buses. Known as prepping, this gives the child as much advance notice as possible about an upcoming activity or event. We wanted Mary to be as ready as possible for her upcoming bus rides. We also started talking to Mary about the Whitestone School, how she would be going to "big girl school" now. She seemed to like that term and transitioned extremely well to the new school. In fact, she didn't fuss or hesitate to get on the bus that first morning.

Debby and I were far more emotional, holding back tears while I snapped a half dozen photos of the big, first bus ride. We then jumped in the car and discreetly followed the bus on its route from our house to the school, just to make sure Mary would be OK. We saw her get off the bus and walk right into the school building, so we breathed a sigh of relief and trusted the bus from that day forward. Mary rode the bus to and from the Whitestone School each weekday for the next 15 months including summer school. She liked the bus so much that each day she got up from the breakfast table, put on her coat and backpack and stood by the front door and/or window looking for the bus.

While Mary loved the bus, I was a little self-conscious about it. While I wasn't exactly embarrassed about the bus, I knew it was a pretty obvious sign to everyone in the neighborhood that something must not be right about Mary. For years I had heard people joke about "taking the short bus to school" because that's the kind of bus kids in special education required. Typically developing students usually ride the standard longer buses to and from school and on field trips. But the special education kids ride the short buses, capable of holding only about 15 to 16 students.

It was a put-down and an insult to say to someone that they must have ridden the short bus to school. Though I rarely made such insensitive remarks myself, I remember laughing a few times earlier in my life when someone talked about riding the short bus, and now I felt ashamed. Never again would I laugh at any "short bus" jokes. In fact, I began to notice those short buses throughout the neighborhood more and more often, as various kids and teenagers were picked up and dropped off. Lots of people have challenges, and that includes our family. Now I thank God for the bus drivers and bus assistants who help get all of those special children to school each day. Needless to say I have a keen appreciation for them now.

With the whole transportation issue no longer a concern, we were free to focus on Mary's new school setting. Mary's teacher, Miss D, was a tall, thin, soft-spoken young Caucasian woman with short black hair. Miss D took a liking to Mary right away and took on her new challenge without hesitation. Mary was joined in class by seven other special education students, six boys and a girl, each with varying degrees of disability.

Several students had language delays and several boys were, like Mary, placed on the autism spectrum. In fact, we were hearing more and more about autism all the time. We had front-row seats for a national crisis. Autism rates were beginning to skyrocket as the condition mushroomed from a rare disorder to a major global problem as noted in the introduction to this book.

Debby and I would learn that even with the rapidly rising rates of autism, there was still a much higher percentage of boys diagnosed than girls. (Ratios published online range anywhere from 10 boys to every girl diagnosed to 4 boys for every girl diagnosed. I read several articles online suggesting that because young boys are usually more active and demonstrative than young girls, their autistic attributes tend to be more visible and thus they tend to get diagnosed more frequently.) Mary's entire experience at the Whitestone School was spent with female teachers, female class assistants and male peers, except the one girl in her class who graduated three months after Mary started and moved on to a new school.

The lack of girls in Mary's class concerned Debby and I. Anyone could watch young boys and girls play for five minutes and observe a tremendous difference. We knew that in Mary's class at least, the boys had each other and their similar interests in cars and trains and superhero action figures. Though the boys wouldn't say much to each other and didn't necessarily interact often, they at least had the opportunity to watch other boys playing. This was an opportunity to see, hear and observe how other boys their age played and acted, and that allowed them to potentially modify and regulate their own behaviors.

However, Mary didn't have that same opportunity. She looked around and saw boys playing with cars and trains and action figures. There just wasn't anyone else that looked like her or wanted to play with the doll house. She was pretty much left on her own and couldn't model another girl's behavior if she wanted to once the other girl left the program. Nevertheless, the classroom environment was a step in the right direction compared to the day-care center, so we embraced it and hoped for the best.

To help Mary feel comfortable in class, Miss D and her two assistants created a picture schedule for every conceivable activity. Mary learned to follow the schedule and it seemed to calm her and help her focus much better. Prior to attending the Whitestone School, Mary's only guidelines for the day were verbal instructions from her parents, family and day-care providers. Turns out that Mary didn't always comprehend verbal instructions clearly, and the picture schedule gave her a precise and easily understood roadmap for her day. There were pictures for play time, table time, puzzles, snacks, lunch, art, writing, etc. Sometimes Mary was allowed to help create the schedule, other times she had to follow what the teacher decided. All eight students in the class followed the schedules perfectly, although as Mary grew more comfortable in her surroundings and with her teacher she would occasionally sneak over and rearrange the pictures on the schedule to an order she preferred!

Because Mary joined the Whitestone School in May, she attended for only three months before it was time for the vacation break in August. As we neared the break, we were called in to meet with the Whitestone School's psychologist. The psychologist, a pleasant middle-aged woman, had an easy-going manner and liked to laugh a lot. She clearly enjoyed her work. She had some complimentary things to say about Mary and told us how much everybody enjoyed working with our little girl. She also cautioned us, however, that Mary was screeching quite often and was having trouble staying on task. Because of this, she and Miss D both felt that Mary would need some extra attention during the upcoming school year.

The psychologist recommended we apply for SEIT services to get someone who would come to our house several hours per week to work with Mary one-on-one. A SEIT[7] is a Special Education Itinerant Teacher, certified or licensed to work directly with special needs children. SEITs provide student support in a variety of areas, including speech-language pathology, audiology, interpreting services, physical therapy, occupational therapy and dozens of others. This therapy can be based either in the classroom or at the student's home depending on the circumstances.

In Mary's case, the psychologist said she would recommend finding a SEIT familiar with Applied Behavior Analysis (ABA) therapy, a common treatment for autism. ABA therapy[8] consists of repetitive task completion, after which the student receives a small reward for completing a task successfully. Various studies have shown that young autistic children can make dramatic improvements when undergoing as much as 40 hours of ABA therapy each week. The repetitions and the rewards lead to improved concentration and language skills in many students. Typically, the younger the student is when starting ABA therapy, the better the outcome achieved in terms of improvement of skills.

ABA therapists are often very patient, kind-hearted people. They have the desire to help children despite often being subjected to physical and verbal attacks from frustrated students and buckets of tears from students grinding it out through the hours and hours of repetitive training. I've heard of parents leaving the house or going to the furthest room possible in the house to avoid the shrieking, screaming and crying that often accompany ABA therapy when difficult and/or new skills are introduced. Nevertheless many children have gained markedly improved skills after going through ABA therapy. However, because the work is intense and challenging, ABA therapists are often in short supply.

At first we were disappointed to hear the psychologist's report. We hoped to hear that Mary was picking things up quickly and was the star of her class. Now we were finding out that Mary was happy there but not necessarily making rapid progress. At home we were not seeing much difference in Mary yet, but we knew it was still early. We took the psychologist's advice and set up a meeting with our school district representative that summer. We hoped to get 5 hours per week of service and envisioned someone coming to our house for an hour each day after school. We were cautioned by the Whitestone School psychologist that these requests were often rejected for cost or lack of availability of resources, but Debby and I prayed that Mary would get the help she obviously still needed. Once again our prayers were answered.

When we met with the school district representative and Miss D, we presented our case for increasing Mary's services and waited anxiously for the response. The school rep thought a moment and then said no, 5 hours wouldn't work. She suggested 8 hours per week! She did caution us that it might take several weeks to find a suitable therapist, but she would get to work on it right away. We were elated of course and spent the last few weeks of August enjoying the break from school and looking forward to Mary's pre-Kindergarten year.

In early September, Mary returned to the Whitestone School and we met with the school and district representatives to write an updated IEP for Mary. This would be basically the same stuff that was in her previous IEP, but this one was good for the entire 2005-2006 school year. The major change in Mary's IEP was to add 8 hours per week of at-home ABA therapy from the SEIT to her required services.

Week after week went by and Mary continued to enjoy going to school. We asked periodically about the SEIT and were told that it was difficult finding someone qualified for the position. Every therapy center they contacted was either booked to capacity already or the available therapists did not have the ABA-related background that Mary needed.

At the Whitestone School, Mary's teacher was using ABA concepts to teach Mary. They worked on recognizing letters and identifying the sounds of each letter, identifying numbers, answering yes/no questions consistently, improving social interactions, staying on task and in her seat and sharing items of interest with peers. When Mary responded correctly or exhibited proper behavior, she would receive a reward such as play time with a favored toy or free time to play. Stickers were used to denote appropriate and inappropriate behavior. If the kids did something correctly, they got a rocket sticker. Inappropriate behavior was acknowledged with a cloud sticker. Periodically Mary would give us glimpses into her classroom life by spontaneously saying "Mary gets a rocket," or so-and-so "gets a cloud."

We could see at home that Mary was starting to tolerate interaction with us more than she had in at least a year. She no longer was so quick to leave the room when we were all together. She still didn't talk much, but she was more and more willing to be near us as long as she was doing something she wanted. We took this as a positive step, even though Mary still exhibited screeching when she got excited and continued to be stingy with her language.

Then finally, in late October, we got a call from the school district representative saying they had located a suitable therapist. A young man named Gilbert Lim had been working with several children and had a full schedule, but one of those children was no longer in need of services and Gilbert would be available if we were interested. Of course we jumped at the chance and eagerly awaited our first meeting with Gilbert.

12. Critical At-Home Tutoring

Before meeting Gilbert, I remember thinking how odd it was that we were about to welcome this stranger into our house, and he was going to spend 8 hours per week with us for the better part of the next year. What if we didn't hit it off right away or at all? What if he was overly strict or unfriendly? What if Mary didn't want to have anything to do with him? What if he dressed funny or smelled bad? I mean, this guy was going to come into our house every day and we really needed him to make an impact, and I really wanted to like the guy since I'd have to deal with him on a daily basis.

After exchanging a few voicemails, Gilbert and I finally connected in late October and set up a meeting at our house, a get-to-know-each-other session. There would be no pressure, no tests, no stress. It was an opportunity to get things started on the right foot and an opportunity for Gilbert to assess the challenge that lay in front of him.

When the car pulled up in front of the house, I peered through the curtains with a mix of uncertainty, anxiety, nervousness and excitement. Gilbert got out of the silver sedan, grabbed a bag and a few things out of the backseat then opened the trunk. I wondered what he was up to. What was in the trunk? Gilbert pulled out a large black guitar case, gave the trunk a slam and headed up our steps. So Gilbert was a musician too? I kind of liked that.

From the first time Gilbert walked though our door, it felt like change was in the air. No, he didn't play Bob Dylan's "The Times They Are a-Changin'" on his guitar, but he could have. That's the trust we placed in him, and that's the confidence he carried in himself in a pure and simple way. I quickly sized him up: clean-cut Asian-American young man with short dark hair, comfortably dressed in his garnet polo shirt and khaki slacks, probably about 5-foot-7. He had an easygoing smile on his roundish face. I figured we were close in age; perhaps he was a few years younger, but definitely the same generation. He had a positive air about him and a refreshing outsider's viewpoint that was coming into a situation with confidence and enthusiasm. I thought, "Thank God!" Gilbert passed all the first impression tests. Now, most importantly, what would Mary think of him?

Mary came over to meet Gilbert and of course didn't say much. His "bag of tricks" caught her attention right away though and without hesitation Gilbert pulled a few instructional toys out of his bag. There were puzzles and colorful stacking objects and books and games. Charlie came over and sat down by Mary and they started stacking some blocks and pulling more and more things out of the bag. Gilbert never complained, never got upset, even when all of his stuff ended up all over the floor. He was excited to see Mary's interest and observed a few words spoken between Mary and Charlie.

The awkward first few minutes passed quickly and before long Gilbert was on the floor with Mary and Charlie doing a puzzle. Mary hadn't shown interest in puzzles in over a year but all of a sudden she was sitting with Gilbert and completing a puzzle! I stayed in the background and minutes passed into an hour. Finally Gilbert opened the guitar case and strummed a few songs. He had a happy and innocent look on his face as he played classic kids' songs like "Old McDonald" and "Twinkle, Twinkle Little Star." Right from that first day Mary stayed with Gilbert and listened to the songs, even though she didn't sing along yet.

"I use music as another tool to get through to kids," Gilbert explained as he started to pack up his things. "Some kids really respond."

"I think this is going to work out well," Gilbert continued. "I just have to finish up some paperwork on the child who just left. I should have that cleared up in two weeks and then we can get started."

"Ugh, two more weeks," I thought. I had all this excitement and positive energy flowing and now we were going to have to wait two weeks? Of course we had no other options at that point, so we agreed that Gilbert would start in early November and would join us every Monday through Thursday from 4:30 p.m. to 6:30 p.m. We had actually preferred an earlier time slot, more of an after-school timing, but we were happy to be moving forward and Gilbert seemed like a good person.

One of Gilbert's first steps was to set up a picture schedule, similar to what Mary was using at the Whitestone School. He told us this was an element of the TEACCH method, which was established in the early 1970s in North Carolina. TEACCH, which stands for Treatment and Education of Autistic and related Communication Handicapped Children, is actually a wide-ranging program that uses various methods and strategies to help special needs individuals depending on their capabilities.[9]

Gilbert laminated a piece of paper about 6 inches wide by 12 inches long with the word "Mary" across the top. This was to be the picture holder. Down the middle of the laminated page he put a strip of Velcro. He then went to a website (there are numerous) with all kinds of pictures for various activities. There were pictures of stick-figure people brushing their teeth, eating food, drinking, combing hair and doing other routine daily tasks. There were also dozens of pictures of activities such as writing, reading, music, math, spelling, puzzles, games, table top activities, etc. Each of the pictures was about 2 inches by 2 inches and laminated, with Velcro on the back. All of the picture cards were placed in a small bag attached to the bottom of the picture holder. These were the components of Mary's at-home picture schedule, and Mary and Gilbert went over each of the pictures quite a few times until Mary knew what every picture represented.

Each day when Gilbert arrived, he said hello to everyone and then took 4 or 5 pictures from the bag and lined them up on the scheduler. Then Mary would know how she was going to spend the next two hours of her day. There would be no surprises and no difficult transitions. Each activity was timed, and when the timer went off or when a task was completed (such as finishing a puzzle) it was time to put that activity picture back in the bag and move on to the next activity. On a typical day, Mary's schedule might start with Gilbert reading her a book, then moving to the floor to complete a puzzle, then sitting at her little desk and counting some blocks or other objects, then writing at the desk, then music, then dinner, then finally arts and crafts.

We always timed the lesson so that I had dinner ready at 6 p.m., and Mary and Charlie ate together. Initially, Gilbert incorporated behavior therapy into the meal routine. He created a picture grid showing different types of foods, as well as pictures of a plate, fork, spoon and cup. When Mary sat down to eat each night, she had a blank table in front of her. Gilbert would hold up the grid and ask Mary what she wanted. Mary had to ask for a plate – only when she spoke up and asked for a plate loud enough for all of us to hear did she get a plate put in front of her. (At first Gilbert had to point to the picture that he wanted Mary to identify, but before long she caught on and asked for what she needed without Gilbert needing to point out each item.) Then Gilbert asked what else Mary needed, and she would ask for a fork, a cup, etc.

I always had the food cooked and waiting in separate bowls on the counter near the table so that once Mary had her plate and utensils in front of her she could then identify the foods. Gilbert would ask what was for dinner, and I would put the first bowl on the table. Mary would look at the bowl and say "broccoli" or whatever was there. Then she would get a scoop. Then she would identify the next food and so on until she had a little of each item (whether she wanted to eat everything or not, she had to ask for some of everything before she was permitted to start eating).

This process took a good 10-15 minutes the first few weeks, and everybody got a little impatient looking at the food but not eating it. But Mary quickly understood that the faster she responded to Gilbert's questions correctly, the sooner she would be given her food and be allowed to eat. It was an incredibly effective way of getting Mary to interact with us and verbalize her wants and needs with us every day. Once the kids finally started eating, Gilbert went into the living room to set up the arts and crafts project for the day.

After the nightly dinner routine, Mary would finish eating and then go in the other room to create an art project. Art projects usually followed the traditional holiday themes for each month, and Gilbert often used art to bring books to life such as Eric Carle's *The Very Hungry Caterpillar.*

Progress was rapid and noticeable. By the middle of December, Mary could trace her name on a large piece of lined paper. She didn't always hold the pen correctly, but they worked on that and her tracing got better and better. As the tracing progressed, Gilbert started writing letters or numbers on one line, then would skip a line and write letters or numbers on the third line. Mary would then write freehand on lines 2 and 4 what she saw on lines 1 and 3 above. It was messy at first but got better and better. By mid-January, Gilbert was ecstatic. For the first time in her life, and nearly a full year after she was diagnosed with autism, Mary sat down at her desk and wrote her name, correctly, without tracing it! Debby and I were so proud. We took that little strip of paper and hung it up in the kitchen above the doorway where we would see it every day. It stayed there all year, a reminder as to where Mary was and where she was going.

One of Gilbert's secrets to success was his flexibility in working with Mary. He didn't try to force her to one specific method of learning. Instead, he got to know Mary and assessed that she had great untapped skills. He sensed that Mary had the ability to function at a much higher level but just didn't have the confidence and interest in doing so.

Gilbert took me aside one day, after perhaps a month of working with Mary, and said he was deviating somewhat from classic ABA therapy because Mary didn't need it. He said she demonstrated an ability to complete tasks fairly well when given a proper motivator and fortunately didn't need the constant repetition. This is one of the peculiarities of the autism spectrum; despite sharing many challenges, every child is affected differently. Some desperately need the repetition, whereas it bored Mary to the point where she wouldn't cooperate. So instead of following the rote ABA methods, Gilbert borrowed the reward component and used it at his discretion.

Mary's therapy rewards were typically M&M's or Goldfish crackers. When she saw either of those items, it was amazing how cooperative and willing to work she became! Completing a puzzle might be worth two M&M's. Tracing her name and phone number three times might be worth six Goldfish crackers. Sitting still on the couch next to Gilbert as he read a picture book, and answering comprehension/observation questions about the book might be worth six M&Ms, and so on. This method really worked with Mary.

Though we weren't crazy about her M&M intake, we were thrilled with the results. Within a few months of Gilbert's home therapy, Mary was willing to sit and listen as someone read her a book, either Gilbert or her parents. She was doing puzzles again. We would give her some blank paper and a pen and she would draw a smiley face or write her name. We still weren't having conversations with Mary, but she was more and more interested in interacting with us. She was finally showing signs of academic ability by answering questions from the books Gilbert read, writing letters and numbers, counting objects, etc.

By the middle of February, Mary had completed three months of therapy with Gilbert. We were ready for a vacation, so Debby and I took the kids to California for a week. The highlight of the trip was a visit to Disneyland. We knew it would be crowded during President's Week but we knew the kids would enjoy it. They had a great time, but what I remember most was sitting in our hotel room near the park one evening. We had just finished a half day in Disneyland and a half day of swimming at the hotel pool. The kids loved it, as we thought. Debby and I ordered some snacks from room service and we all sat around relaxing and playing with some souvenir toys. All of a sudden there was a knock on the door – room service. Before any of us could say anything, Mary said aloud "WHO'S AT THE DOOR?" My head spun around so fast I almost got whiplash! I jumped up and down and pointed at Debby.

"Did you hear that?" I asked and exclaimed. "Did you hear that?"

It was the first time in at least two years that Mary had asked a question. To the best of our recollection Mary had asked some basic "Can I" questions before she regressed, but she certainly had never asked a "WH" question. That is always something the evaluators would ask of us – "Does Mary ask and/or understand WH questions: who, what, where, when and why." And we could never answer affirmatively until that late afternoon in a Disneyland hotel room. All of the therapy at school and at home with Gilbert was working! Mary was becoming slightly more aware of her surroundings, returning slowly from "her world" and back into ours. We were getting glimpses here and there of our daughter again, and I knew then that finding Mary was possible.

13. Choosing the Right Kindergarten

Mary spent the rest of the 2005-2006 school year attending the Whitestone School in the mornings and working with Gilbert in the late afternoons. In between we took many trips to the park around the corner for fresh air and exercise. Mary made a beeline for the swing sets every time and would spend a half hour on the swings nearly every day. There was something about the back and forth sensation on the swing that stimulated her and drew her back to those swings every time.

While Mary kept busy with her school work and therapy, Debby and I turned our attention to Kindergarten. At a "Turning 5" welcome to Kindergarten assembly for special education parents in October, we had heard a brief mention about a relatively new program that was being introduced in Queens by the New York City Department of Special Education. The Autism Nest Program was developed in collaboration between the Department of Education and New York University's Institute for Education & Social Policy. The ASD Nest Program[10] was already underway at a few schools in Brooklyn and Manhattan, and to our delight, Queens was getting its first Nest Program for Kindergarten in September 2006, the very year that Mary was starting Kindergarten.

The basic idea of the Nest program was to take 4 high-functioning autistic children and put them in a classroom with up to 8 typically developing children who would act as positive role models. The class would be taught by two full-time teachers, each of whom would receive training on working with autistic children prior to the start of the school year. A brochure for the ASD Nest program noted, "in addition to the standard academic curriculum, specialized curricula and instructional strategies to foster relationship development, adaptive skills, language and communication development and sensory/motor development are infused throughout the day, thus minimizing the need to service children outside the classroom." (As the children grow older and progress through the program, class sizes get slightly larger at higher grade levels.) We were told to submit our contact information to some special education representatives there at the meeting and stay tuned for more information in the months to come.

At the time I remember thinking it was like they were talking directly to me. From the first moment I heard the news about the program I knew Mary was going to be a part of it. In fact, I went home that very night and started a 9-day Novena to St. Joseph, asking that Mary be successfully admitted to the Autism Nest Program. I then left it in God's hands. Debby and I jumped through a half dozen hoops for the school district to help make it happen. But we didn't know if Mary was accepted into the Nest program until very late in the spring.

As we took Mary to various tests and evaluations for the Nest program, we were receiving mixed reports on Mary's progress at the

Whitestone School. On the positive side, Mary was demonstrating an enthusiasm for school and for certain school activities. She was sounding out letters and writing a little better. She was following a picture schedule and showing increased responsibility for the rules of the classroom. All of the rules, that is, except staying in her seat and on task during her non-preferred activities. And, unfortunately, she was still echoing dialogue from televisions shows regularly and screeching when she got excited.

At first we downplayed these shortcomings. Of course she gets out of her seat; she's got autism, we rationalized. Of course she echoes dialogue from television; she's got autism, we rationalized. Of course she screeches when she's excited; she's got autism, we once again rationalized. We were getting good at rationalizing and answering for Mary. It was a deeply ingrained habit for us at that point. But we figured that anybody who worked with special education children would understand and look the other way when Mary screeched, echoed or got out of her seat.

Gilbert, who enjoyed the luxury of having one-on-one interaction in the comfort of Mary's home, was more tolerant of Mary's screeching and restlessness. He asked Debby and me for our thoughts on breaking those habits of Mary's, but whatever we tried had very little impact. To Gilbert, the shortcomings were inconvenient but were not going to bring him down or dampen his positivism. For Mary's teacher and assistants at the Whitestone School, however, the shortcomings were disruptive to the class. It wasn't so bad that Mary was ever in jeopardy of losing her spot in the school, but it was detrimental enough that Mary consistently got marked down for those shortcomings in her progress reports. It was bad enough that her teacher and the psychologist worried about how Mary would fit into a larger Kindergarten classroom.

In May we learned that Mary had been accepted into the Autism Nest Program. We were thrilled and excited for Mary. She was going to be given every opportunity to succeed: a small class size, two full-time teachers, positive role models and three peers who, like her, were on the autism spectrum. We found out later where the program was to be located and who would teach it, but at least the anxiety about where Mary was headed in the fall was cleared. St. Joseph had pulled this one out for us and we were grateful.

In late June, the Whitestone School held its graduation ceremony. They decorated the gymnasium in the basement and rolled out a stage. Everything had a 1950s sock-hop Rock-and-Roll theme. The parents sat in folding chairs holding cameras and ceremony programs. At first it seemed a little over the top for 4-year olds, but when the children started processing into the gym wearing their royal blue robes and caps it really hit me. Along came Mary with her cap and gown, following along with her classmates as the traditional graduation march song played. The lump in my throat and tears in my eyes took me completely by surprise. I looked at Debby and she had tears too. It was OK to be emotional, for we knew how much work had gone into getting Mary ready for this day.

As the kids strolled up to the stage and took their places, a flood of memories washed over me. I recalled those evaluations done at the school less than a year and half earlier, when Mary wouldn't talk to us and wouldn't tolerate being in the same room with us. I remembered getting our first big break when a spot suddenly opened up at the Whitestone School the previous spring. I remembered that sunny May morning when we walked Mary to the school bus for the first time and watched her being driven off in someone else's hands for the first time. I remembered sitting through parent support group meetings at the school, where I learned that Debby and I really weren't the only ones dealing with these issues; other parents struggled each day to get their kids dressed and fed as well. I remembered the meetings with the psychologist and the concern about Mary's shortcomings.

Mary still had a long way to go. As the kids walked up to the stage that graduation day, Mary held her speech therapist's hand so she wouldn't bolt off in another direction. And once they got on stage, Mary clutched a small *Dora* doll the entire time to help keep her grounded and comfortable. At times I noticed the speech therapist gently holding Mary's shoulders from behind to keep her in place.

As the majority of kids sang a few classic 1950s songs such as Bobby Day's "Rockin Robin," Mary mostly just looked around and smiled. She danced a little, sang a little, and it was quite a moment, tears and all. Mary was participating in the moment, but she was struggling with it and not really understanding the significance of the day. But it was a milestone for us, and we framed her diploma and put several graduation photos in a collage frame and finally felt good about our daughter's potential. Maybe she would amount to something after all!

We still go to the church next door, and Charlie plays basketball every winter weekend in that same gymnasium. In fact, Charlie now attends Holy Trinity Elementary School in that very building and I coach the third grade boys' basketball team. And every so often I stand there in the gym and in my mind I picture that stage and hear those sock hop songs and see our special little girl up on that stage and I get choked up all over again.

14. Brotherly Love Not Always Easy

As summer rolled along, we knew our days with Gilbert were drawing to a close. One of the requirements of the Autism Nest Program was that children were not allowed to have outside professional influences on their education because so many services were provided in the program. With a lot of money, training and time going into the development of the Nest program, everyone involved with it needed to be able to gauge the success of the program on its own, not speculate how much of Mary's progress might be attributed to a home therapist. Also, if a student required SEIT services, he or she in all likelihood wasn't qualified for the Nest program.

Our excitement and enthusiasm for the Nest program was almost evenly matched by our devotion to and appreciation of Gilbert. We knew we had to look forward, not backward though, and we accepted the position in the Nest program knowing that we'd have to eliminate Mary's sessions with Gilbert by the end of the summer.

By the summer of 2006, Mary was nearly 5-years old. She was writing freehand and interacting with others somewhat, so we saw progress. Though she still did not engage in much conversation, she was far more interactive than ever before and was answering yes/no questions about 75% of the time, quite an improvement from when Gilbert first started working with her. But Mary wasn't the only person thriving from Gilbert's influence. Charlie was a regular participant in the daily home-therapy sessions and picked up as much as Mary did from each of those lessons.

Charlie turned 3 in June 2006 and that summer he was already sounding out letters and writing his name. His writing wasn't great but it was legible and getting better. Charlie was also interacting with Gilbert, listening as Gilbert read to Mary, completing table-top puzzles alongside Mary, etc. Charlie was like a sponge taking in all of this instruction. He learned to read by age 4 and completed first-grade level math and reading comprehension work in pre-Kindergarten. Clearly the benefits of Gilbert's teaching were not limited to Mary!

Charlie's intelligence is a gift from God I believe. It's one of God's ways of compensating Charlie for all the challenges that go along with growing up with an autistic sibling. Living with Mary has been frustrating many times for Charlie. I cannot begin to count how many times Charlie asked Mary a question that she didn't answer. She just flat-out ignores him sometimes. This was really bad a few years ago, when Charlie first started talking, and it continues to be a source of frustration at times to Charlie. He has had to live with autism his whole life and only recently has he begun to know and understand what *autism* means.

Those nights when Mary woke up and echoed television dialogue had to bother Charlie, since the two of them shared a bedroom for three years and Mary's echolalia sometimes was loud enough to wake him up.

Every so often Charlie would shuffle into our bedroom exhausted and upset that Mary was making so much noise and he couldn't sleep.

Additionally, Mary often needed more attention than she would otherwise have received if she was typically developing. Because Mary has a tendency to wander off, Debby and I have to constantly keep track of Mary's exact whereabouts. This means that when Charlie and I are kicking a soccer ball in the back yard, I have to stop every 5-10 minutes to "go check on Mary." Charlie heard me say that a thousand times. So his activity gets disrupted for a few minutes on a regular basis while we check on his sister.

Then there are gatherings with family and friends. At first it was cute when Mary recited dialogue. But now that she's 8-years old and growing taller and bigger, it doesn't seem so cute. It's embarrassing to Charlie when cousins or friends ask why Mary keeps talking about *Elmo* or *Dora*, subjects other kids left behind years ago. Charlie usually just shrugs it off but occasionally he'll comment that Mary's autism bothers him.

When Charlie turned 4, we explained to him that Mary has something called autism and it makes her brain work a little differently than most everyone else's. That's why she has two teachers and he has only one. And that's why Mary repeats things so often and why sometimes she doesn't answer when he asks her a question. It's why she eats different foods than us sometimes and why she sometimes has tantrums over what seem like little things to us. Charlie nodded his head and sort of understood. For the next few days he asked questions and seemed to get the general idea: Mary is special and smart, she just doesn't think the way we do all the time.

For the most part, Charlie has dealt with Mary's autism with acceptance and understanding. The kids fight over things now and then, like any other siblings, but he has really helped Mary simply by providing typical role modeling for her whenever she's home. Charlie is always there to play with when she wants to and they often do interact. He's her favorite duck-duck-goose playmate, and they often sit together and play trains or watch television or build towers out of blocks or Legos®. And during those hours of playtime Mary often asks Charlie to play with her or she makes comments to Charlie about what they're doing. When Charlie learned how to whistle, that new talent fascinated Mary and she asked Charlie to whistle for her frequently. All things considered, Charlie has been a huge help in Mary's development, and Mary's special education needs have helped shape Charlie and benefited him in many ways too.

Gilbert's work with Mary came to an end in late August as scheduled. We dreaded the upcoming cutoff date, knowing the services would not be approved beyond August 31. As always, Gilbert, Mary and Charlie spent the summer working puzzles, writing letters and numbers, counting and creating arts and crafts. I will always remember Gilbert for the enthusiasm and dedication he showed to Mary and Charlie for those 10 months. But perhaps mostly, I'll remember the music.

As I wrote earlier, the daily schedule always concluded with dinner and an art project. It also always included music just before dinner; that way, if I needed an extra few minutes to get dinner ready, Gilbert just played a few more songs and stretched that activity out. It was always the highlight of the session for Mary, and I think for Gilbert, too. During the course of those 10 months, I talked to Gilbert about music and guitars often. He owns a half-dozen guitars and attends gatherings for guitar aficionados on a regular basis.

But as Gilbert noted when he first met Mary, music really brought the two of them together. In the early days, Gilbert would randomly go through a few songs and Mary would bob her head along to the music. He then laminated some cards, similar to the picture schedule cards, with each card representing a different song. The music evolved to the point where Mary and Charlie took turns picking out a song card and placing it at Gilbert's feet. He would play that song while the children took turns picking out the next song.

Mary's head bobbing to the music gradually improved to acting out the various parts of songs, such as the spider going up the water spout and rain coming down, washing the spider out. This activity evolved further to where Mary actually sang the songs with Gilbert and acted them out. The power of that guitar! It was like Gilbert had turned back the clock three years to when Mary sang and danced for us all the time. Now we were doing more than just living with the autism, we were getting to enjoy seeing Mary sing and dance again.

Every music session had one specific song included at some point: "Here Comes the Sun" by the Beatles. It started as a joke. Mary handed Gilbert the card for "Mr. Golden Sun" and Gilbert played "Here Comes the Sun" instead. I laughed and Gilbert nodded, then he played the "Mr. Golden Sun" song. A few minutes later, while the kids were eating, I heard Gilbert playing "Here Comes the Sun" again. I walked into the other room and told Gilbert how great that sounded, so he played it again. By this time Mary and Charlie were done eating and also came to listen to Gilbert play. Everyone got a kick out of it and loved to hear that song. As a result, Mary asked Gilbert to play "Here Comes the Sun" every day from that day forward.

Finally the days ran out and it was time to say goodbye to Gilbert. We met for dinner at a steakhouse nearby for one last get-together and to thank Gilbert for his incredible achievements. The meal was a bit chaotic as Mary had trouble sitting still in her seat and Charlie spilled a drink, but overall it was fun to hang out with Gilbert outside the house. Next to the steakhouse was a large bookstore, and Debby and I took the kids to the bookstore after dinner to pick out a few of the books that we loved reading with Gilbert. We stepped outside and Debby hugged Gilbert. Then Gilbert and I did the handshake-pull-in-man-hug and said thanks and goodbye. My heart sank as I watched him walk away. With Gilbert everything had always been positive and happy, and yet now we had to move forward without him. Debby and I told ourselves that there was another family out there desperately seeking help, and now Gilbert would walk into their lives, guitar in hand, ready to turn that family around too.

15. Another Baby and Our New Approach to Vaccines

A week after saying goodbye to Gilbert, we said hello to Martin James Robertson, our third child. Marty was born September 8, 2006, the first week of Mary's Kindergarten year in the Autism Nest Program. Marty was like a bonus to Debby and me, an extra child to hold and treasure. Most of our family and friends assumed we were done having kids when Charlie was born, since we had our girl and our boy. Then with Mary's autism diagnosis, most people thought we definitely had our hands full and wouldn't take on the responsibility of a third child. And there was an unspoken but real understanding that having a third child put us in the situation of possibly caring for two autistic kids if the new baby didn't develop typically. Debby and I never actually spoke those concerns out loud, perhaps not wanting to jinx ourselves or the baby.

Mary and Charlie came to the hospital to meet baby Marty the day after he was born, and immediately we noticed a big difference in Mary's attention to the baby. Recall that when Charlie was born, Mary was completely indifferent to him. With Marty though, Mary immediately showed an interest in the little newcomer. She said "Hi, Marty" right away and snuggled up in the hospital bed with Debby and Marty. Charlie elbowed his way into the group as well and the three of them spent a good hour cuddling up in the bed gazing at their baby brother.

Once we got Marty home, Mary continued to show enthusiasm for her littlest brother. She would grab a blanket and drape it over him while Debby or I were holding him.

"Marty wants a blanket," Mary would declare.

Other times Mary would pick up Marty's bottle and somewhat hastily try to put it in his mouth.

"Marty needs a drink," Mary would say, or "Marty needs his bottle."

Debby and I were pleased to see Mary's interactions with Marty. She had come a long way in three years. Despite Mary's many shortcomings, we saw this interaction as a sign that Mary was headed in the right direction.

More recently, as Marty passed his third birthday, he met all the developmental milestones. He talked all the time, made regular eye contact, asked questions all the time and was interested in interacting frequently with his family. He ate everything we put in front of him and did not have any bowel issues that we could see at that point. In other words, Marty was typically developing and not on the autism spectrum.

Debby and I took precautions though. In our minds, there was enough uncertainty over whether vaccines contribute to autism that we played it cautiously with Marty. The Measles-Mumps-Rubella (MMR) vaccine in particular has been cited by many parents as the trigger for their child's autism. It was not uncommon to hear parents say that before the MMR shot, their child was fine; after the MMR shot, the child regressed rapidly. Much of the medical community completely denied any correlation between vaccines and autism though.

The Centers for Disease Control and Prevention and the World Health Organization have concluded that the MMR vaccine does not cause autism, based on various large studies.[11] But as I said, many families affected by autism disagree or at least hold onto a degree of caution. Anecdotal evidence was mounting across the country (on television programs and the Internet) of cases of typically developing children regressing into shells of their former selves soon after receiving the MMR shots. There are countless pages on the Internet devoted to this vaccination controversy, which goes well beyond the scope of this book.

In mid-2008, entertainment stars Jenny McCarthy and Jim Carrey led a march in Washington, D.C. from the Washington Monument to the Capitol building. There McCarthy, who has a recovered autistic son, and several other speakers called for a new vaccination schedule that would spread out the vaccinations over a longer period of time. On her website, www.generationrescue.org, McCarthy noted that in 1983 the recommended vaccination schedule contained just 10 shots, and by 2007 the recommended vaccination schedule produced by the Centers for Disease Control and Prevention had swelled to 36! McCarthy also called for greener vaccines; that is, vaccines that are completely free of toxins and preservatives that can potentially harm children.

Charlie had received both the first MMR vaccination and later the MMR booster with no ill effects. At the time of his first MMR vaccine, we weren't aware that Mary had autism and we didn't have reason to question Charlie getting the full MMR immunization. When it came time for his booster though, we were in full autism mode with Mary, and well aware of the MMR debate that was beginning to play out in the media. Nevertheless, Charlie had shown so much social skills and other intellectual abilities that we agreed to just go ahead with the MMR again. It was painful to me to see it happen though, and I nervously watched him like a hawk for the next few days to see if he showed any adverse effects. Thankfully he did not.

Nevertheless, with one child already on the autism spectrum, we weren't taking any chances with Marty. When it came time for Marty's MMR shot at 12 months, we asked that the pediatrician separate his shots and do them individually several months apart. Our pediatricians (there are four doctors sharing an office) were completely OK with our decision and directed us to a compounding pharmacy where we could get the first vaccine filled. So Marty got his measles shot at 13 months and his mumps shot at 16 months.

We are still awaiting Marty's rubella shot, however. We called several local compounding pharmacies and were told that the supply of individual rubella vaccines had been depleted and that they would not be available for at least another 14 months! The same thing was happening with the supply of individual measles and mumps vaccines as well, although that didn't affect us because Marty already had received those shots. In September 2009, one compounding pharmacy provided me a phone number to call one of the drug companies, a vaccine provider, to inquire directly about the availability of the vaccines. A drug company representative told me over the telephone that the company was not currently making the individual measles, mumps or rubella vaccines, but had plans to start again in the next 1-2 years! She encouraged me to call back regularly in case that schedule changed. Clearly, people had been taking notice of the MMR controversy and opting to avoid any risks by separating the vaccines, to the extent that manufacturers could not keep up with demand.

Neither Debby nor I ever claimed the MMR shots directly caused Mary's autism. She didn't seem to become autistic overnight after the immunization; it was a gradual but steady regression. However, knowing more now than we did when Mary was younger, an alternative vaccination schedule for Mary may have been a good idea. Vaccines are important, and it's entirely possible to spread them out and still achieve the benefits vaccines provide and *perhaps* lessen the chances of harming your child. We have come to believe that *too many* immunizations are being given *too soon,* and that some children do not have strong enough immune systems to handle it. As a result, they get sickly and weak from immunizations. That, along with other toxins in food and in the environment, seems to be wreaking havoc on a growing number of children's little bodies and impairing brain function.

16. The ASD Nest Program

That first week of September in 2006 was quite eventful. In addition to Marty's birth, Mary started Kindergarten in the Autism Nest Program. The school district decided to locate the class at Public School 186, also known as Castlewood Elementary, in nearby Bellerose, NY, about a 10-minute drive from our house. We were ecstatic about the location, thrilled that it was so close to home. Earlier in the summer Mary's new teachers had come to our house for a one-hour, get-to-know-Mary session, that gave us a positive first impression.

For teachers to come to our house and sit in our living room with Mary in July showed us the kind of care and attention that everyone was giving to the ASD Nest Program. Mary showed nominal interest in the teachers at that meeting, but at least she cooperated and interacted with them at that point. It made the first few days of school much easier knowing that Mary already had some familiarity with her teachers. To further facilitate a smooth transition, I took Mary and Charlie to the playground at Castlewood several times in the weeks before school started, so Mary got used to seeing the building and making that drive.

Once school began, we were pleased to find out that Mary's class would contain another girl with high-functioning autism. Belinda (not her real name) was much more talkative and outgoing than Mary, but she had enough autistic traits to qualify for the program and was placed in Mary's class. There were actually two ASD Nest classes starting at Castlewood at that time, each with 4 autistic kids and 8 typical kids. They put Mary and Belinda together so the girls would have much more interaction time, while the other class had 4 autistic boys. There were also two autistic boys in Mary's class, Ben and Jack (not his real name).

Very quickly Mary, Belinda, Ben and Jack got to know each other and developed a bit of camaraderie with one another. Each day they would spend an hour going through group speech therapy. The sessions were often very animated and sometimes included physical activity as well. They all loved participating in the sessions and had a great time. The teachers also loved participating in the sessions and sometimes they took pictures of the activity and emailed them to the parents to give us a glimpse at what they were doing. It was a very open and warm environment, with the teachers freely sharing feedback each day after school and inviting parents into the classroom on a regular basis to observe and/or participate in various class activities.

The eight typically developing kids in Mary's class embraced Mary immediately and befriended her. Unfortunately I often observed Mary ignoring her classmates or barely acknowledging their invitations to talk or play, so she had a ways to go in her social interactions. But we knew that going in, and Mary's limited responsiveness didn't seem to dampen the other kids' enthusiasm. They still continued to engage Mary in conversation and to offer invitations to play and interact with them.

As the year progressed, we started to get mixed reviews from Mary's teachers. In fact, they repeatedly stressed how much they adored Mary but were having trouble figuring her out. Turns out Mary's inability to stay seated for longer periods of time, first noted at the Whitestone School, was continuing to be a disrupting factor. When Mary liked an activity, she stuck with it and did well. When teachers asked her to switch gears to another activity, Mary often didn't want to go along with them and would get up and wander around the classroom. We figured this was somewhat to be expected, after all these were autistic kids with challenging behaviors. However, the expectation was that Mary would learn the appropriate behavior within a reasonable amount of time and that didn't seem to be happening. More often than not, one of the teachers would end up paying Mary a lot of one-on-one time while the other teacher took care of the other 11 kids in the class.

Mary was also having some other issues. She had bathroom troubles at least once a week. Mary was potty trained, but she often had trouble wiping correctly after a bowel movement and occasionally required an underwear change due to poor wiping. Mary also passed gas somewhat frequently, which the teachers obviously did not appreciate. This was brought to our attention on a few occasions and we were somewhat indifferent to a degree, not really knowing what we were supposed to do about it!

And then there were the Band-aids. Mary had seen an episode of *Blue's Clues* on television during which the main character Steve draws a Band-aid on his handy-dandy notebook. For the next two months, Mary drew Band-aids whenever she was given paper and a pen or pencil. She was supposed to draw pictures and label them, something they did in class several times a week.

For example, if the theme of the day was apples, the kids had to draw an apple or an apple tree and then label it with the word A-P-P-L-E. Most of the kids did this with varying degrees of competence, except Mary. All she would do was draw Band-aids. Occasionally she would draw the correct subject but then draw a Band-aid next to it!

The teachers were somewhat frustrated at Mary's lack of willingness to follow instructions. They were relieved and surprised a few months later when Mary seemed to grow out of the Band-aid obsession and finally started being more cooperative.

By January 2007, the teachers were running out of ideas on how to address Mary's out-of-seat behavior. On one hand they noted her academic improvements and her warmth and enthusiasm for the teachers and her classmates. However, they were perplexed as to how to get her to stay seated during non-preferred activities. Also, they gave Mary a mandated first-grade readiness test in January and Mary did not do well. She didn't respond to all of the questions, and didn't have all the appropriate behaviors mastered. At that point that we were told that Mary's promotion to first grade was in question and that she had to make some dramatic improvements in the winter and spring or she would not be going to first grade in the fall of 2007.

We were somewhat taken aback at this turn of events. All we ever wanted was for Mary to get into this program, and now Mary was on the verge of blowing it for herself. We saw her making academic improvements but she didn't always demonstrate this at school. For example, we worked with Mary on memorizing sight words, such as A, The, Is, Me, He, With, etc., and by January she had memorized about 40 words. At school, though, they were concerned that she had only memorized a handful of words. Mary was showing these skills at home but not at school, and of course the teachers could only assess Mary based on what they saw in class.

Despite Mary's struggles with some aspects of the program, she did excel in other areas. She and Belinda became friends, often hugging or holding hands. This was a big step for Mary, who had had so little interaction with girls due to the prevalence of boys in her special education classes. Belinda often doted on Mary and was very sweet and in fact helped keep Mary in line at times. We were happy to see Mary and Belinda getting closer, but there were limits. Mary didn't always verbally respond to Belinda's invitations to play or interact, but she usually went along with Belinda anyway. As always, there was progress noted but more work to do!

By early spring, Mary was getting better about staying with the group, although she still had room for improvement. The teachers still had to spend too much time with Mary one-on-one. Mary's screeching had lessened somewhat but she still had too much echolalia at inappropriate times. When she got into echolalia mode, it was like Mary was retreating to her own world again and wouldn't come out for several minutes. She was learning to control the echolalia somewhat though, which we took as a positive sign.

Also, Mary was starting to pay more attention during class field trips and special outings. During a trip to the Bronx Zoo, the kids all gathered in a classroom at the zoo and listened as a zoo keeper talked about various animals. Mary stayed put and paid attention the whole time. One of the class parents who went on the trip made a point to tell us how good Mary was during the session and how nice it was to see her stay engaged on the topic in front of her.

A bigger breakthrough was the dramatic improvement in Mary's hair cutting routine. For the previous three years, including the darkest years of Mary's autism, each and every haircut drained and depressed Mary and me. No amount of prepping or "priming" seemed to work; as soon as Mary got in the barber seat she tensed up and became uncooperative.

Each haircut ended up the same way – I would climb into the chair, hold Mary in my lap and restrain her arms. The sympathetic hair cutter would then do her best to trim Mary's bangs and the back of her hair. Forget about combing out any knots or tangles; that was not happening. Mary would turn bright red, cry loudly and struggle with all of her strength against me trying to escape the haircut. The ordeal would last five or six minutes, then with Mary and me both out of breath, I'd tell the hair cutter we were done. I'd give her an extra large tip for her troubles and walk with Mary back to the car completely bummed out and exhausted.

Midway through Mary's Kindergarten year at Castlewood, Debby took Mary to the salon where she gets her hair cut. Debby had mentioned to Irene, her hairstylist, our struggles with Mary's haircuts, and Irene said all kids are like that and she would be happy to cut Mary's hair. Debby never mentioned that Mary was autistic, however. Debby's motherly intuition told her that Mary needed a fresh, new setting if we ever were to move forward, so Irene was our next best hope. The first time Debby left with Mary for a haircut with Irene, I said a quick prayer and hoped for the best. I actually expected Debby to come back all flustered and perhaps even crying about the painful experience. To my astonishment, that was not to be the case.

As Mary was progressing in her speech and academics, she was also moving forward in her sensory tolerance. We never saw it manifested in her haircuts though because she kept going to the same place where she had so many bad memories. But as soon as Debby took Mary to a new hair salon, the results were different. Though the first haircut with Irene was somewhat challenging, it was manageable. Mary actually allowed Irene to comb her hair. Irene, a young woman with wavy brown hair and a cheerful disposition, patiently worked out the tangles in Mary's hair and assessed her challenge. Debby stood next to Irene and waited for the worst, but Mary hung in there. Debby handed Mary a second and then a third lollipop, and watched as Mary flinched and jerked her head as Irene cut her hair.

Meanwhile at home I was a nervous wreck. So when I saw the car pull into the driveway a mere 15 minutes after they left, I braced for the worst. Such a quick trip had to mean one thing: Mary completely objected and ran out of the salon! Then I saw Mary get out of the car, and her hair was noticeably shorter and she was holding another lollipop. Then Debby got out of the car and flashed a huge grin. The experience, as I described above, was completely tolerable for everyone!

Debby happily took over managing the haircuts, bringing Mary to Irene every other month from that point onward. Each time Mary got more comfortable with Irene and completely cooperated. By the fifth or sixth visit, Debby no longer even went to the chair with Mary. The two of them would walk in together and Mary would go straight to the counter for a lollipop, then to Irene's chair, while Debby sat in the front of the shop. No screaming, no red face, no struggles. To top it all off, the cost at the salon was half the price we had paid those previous years at that children's boutique salon where we had so many struggles. Things had progressed to the point where on a recent visit to Irene, Debby took all three of our kids along and to her amazement, Mary was the best behaved of the three! These days Mary even lets the salon assistant wash her hair and allows Irene to blow dry her hair after the haircut. Unbelievable!

Irene literally transformed our lives with her incredible patience and cheerful attitude. She had only the highest hopes for Mary and wanted to create a great experience for her. Irene succeeded in dramatic fashion, and it wasn't like she used a radical approach or amazing technique. Irene simply showed Mary a warm and welcoming approach and treated her calmly and gently. There was never a "let's roll up the sleeves and get this over with" attitude, so Mary never got too defensive or scared. Instead she looks forward to getting her hair cut now and is completely at ease at the hair salon.

Later that spring, when we had just finished the Autism Speaks "Walk Now For Autism" event in New York City, Debby told Irene about the walk and how emotional the day was for everyone. Irene nodded and listened but seemed a bit puzzled. Finally, she had to ask a question.

"Mary has autism?" Irene asked. "I don't think you ever mentioned that."

Irene's comment was so sincere and so completely welcomed. When Debby got home and relayed the conversation to me, I remember pumping my fist in the air in excitement. For three solid years we had been battling autism. Irene's comment didn't make Mary's autism go away, but it warmed our hearts and felt better than anyone could ever imagine. It gave us hope that Mary was going to be all right, that the days were coming where she wouldn't be defined by her autism.

Of course with Mary, as with any child really, there were always ups and downs. We saw so many positives, but then she would do something to remind us how much work we had left in front of us. For example, in the early spring they conducted mandatory hearing and vision tests at the school. All children were required to participate so the school could assess their sight and vision and address any issues that came up. Unfortunately, Mary did not comply with the testing and didn't understand what was happening. We were given a notice that Mary did not cooperate with the testing and were told that we had to get Mary tested on our own time and those tests would have to be sent in to school.

I called our pediatrician and he agreed to do Mary's hearing test. When I brought Mary in to the pediatrician's office for the test, the doctor was friendly and warm as always. I explained that Mary did not cooperate with the testers at the school so we needed to have a hearing test done. The doctor nodded his head and tried to be sympathetic. He said that of course she did not cooperate given her autism, and unfortunately she never would be able to really cooperate in a situation like that. That comment hit me like a punch in the stomach. I disagreed, but I didn't hold it personally against the doctor. He was just trying to be sympathetic. So I nodded and he proceeded, but that comment stuck with me and I occasionally use it as a personal motivator to keep challenging Mary and pushing her forward. The doctor used an instrument to check Mary's ears. He concluded that her ear was structurally sound, and based on his observations of her he concluded that her hearing was OK. In each of the next two years, Mary was given the hearing tests at school and she cooperated fully and passed the test each time.

17. Piano Lessons Accelerate Recovery

During Mary's Kindergarten year, she and Charlie began taking piano lessons. They played two days a week for 30 minutes apiece. At first Mary was the one taking lessons and Charlie was just there because he had to be, but before long Charlie showed an interest in learning to play the piano too. We thought it would be helpful for Mary to learn to play the piano due to her great memory, her love of music and her ability to thrive in one-on-one situations. Learning to play piano would be a one-on-one process, with Mary and her teacher working together.

We found a great young teacher named Cristiano Tiozzo in the local yellow pages. His listing in the phone book specifically mentioned that he worked with autistic children and children with Attention-Deficit

Disorder. Debby and I were intrigued by this and in late September we met the teacher and started the lessons. It did not go well at first.

Cristiano's piano studio is located in an attached townhouse in a crowded section of Astoria, Queens, about 20 minutes from our house. Parking was challenging at times, so there would be days when we would circle the block two or three times then park a few blocks away and have to walk the rest of the way. Once inside, it only got worse.

Mary would not sit on the piano bench with Cristiano for more than four or five minutes at a time. She sort of paid attention to what he said, but it was obvious that she was not really listening. She seemed more fascinated by his dark rimmed glasses and wavy black hair. Cristiano, who was born and raised in northern Italy, is a sharp dresser who wears European-style clothing including long-sleeve, button-down shirts and pinstriped pants regardless of the weather outside. He does love the piano and working with students, so he gave Mary as much space as possible and looked for at least one positive outcome in every session.

Many times I questioned whether we should continue with the lessons, because Mary's attention span was so short and she was easily distracted. Though she loves music, Mary has an independent streak and often prefers to do her own thing rather than follow along with an instructor. That requires too much self-discipline, so Mary would listen for a short period of time then get agitated and start trying to play whatever notes she wanted. It was quite similar to her approach to swimming lessons.

It was only through Cristiano's incredible patience and willingness to work with Mary that we lasted more than a month. For example, once Mary gets a thought in her head, she cannot focus on anything else until she completes that thought. So, at the piano, if Mary decides she's going to count the keys from one end of the piano to the other, that's what she does. When Cristiano first tried to stop her midway through, Mary resisted and got upset. Cristiano let her continue. Once she finished, she was ready to listen to something new and take instruction. This kind of thing happened all the time. Over time,

Cristiano recognized this and developed a keen awareness of when he could push Mary and when he had to sit back and let her tangent run its course. It was neat to see Cristiano's relationship with Mary grow, and he fully understood the challenge he was accepting. He looked at Mary as a puzzle, something he might solve with many months and years of hard work and perseverance. And she certainly made him work for every positive step they took.

Two to three months into our sessions with Cristiano, Mary would get bored or frustrated and slide off the piano bench and crawl under Cristiano's enormous black grand piano. We would spend a few minutes coaxing her out from under the piano, usually with a handful of Skittles. The routine was somewhat similar to Mary's home therapy sessions, with Cristiano taking on the role previously held by Gilbert. If Mary paid attention and completed a task successfully, she earned a few Skittles. The candy rewards, along with Mary's real interest in music, were enough to keep Mary focused just enough each session to learn something new.

Cristiano's philosophy in teaching piano is not to have the kids memorize a dozen songs and then play the piano in front of an audience. Instead, he prefers to teach his students the basic building blocks of piano playing. So Mary and Charlie first learned to play with their right hand, starting at Middle C. They then learned to play just with the left hand. Then they learned what skips and steps are, etc. After nine months of lessons, they still couldn't really play a full song of any real length, but they were understanding concepts of piano playing. And, amazingly, Mary was starting to read piano music and developing a rapport with Cristiano. It was wonderful to see.

By the nine-month mark, Mary was no longer crawling under the piano and in fact was becoming a wonderful and willing participant. We no longer needed Skittles to help motivate her. She learned "Yankee Doodle" in the spring of 2007 and began playing that all the time. She also started writing short songs. Cristiano would draw a blank music scale and ask Mary to write some notes. Mary would very deliberately write a few notes on the paper and then they would play the song. They would add a few more notes, and then play the song again.

No matter how much progress Mary made though, every time Cristiano introduced a new concept or skill, it pained Mary. You could see it in her body language and in her emotions. The strain of taking on a new and challenging concept hurt, as George Strait has sung in a different context, "it's like wearing a shoe that's too small." That's how Mary reacted, with pain, discomfort and irritation all wrapped together whenever Cristiano pushed her learning curve forward.

To Cristiano's credit, whenever he introduced something new, he expected the pushback and discomfort and worked Mary through it. Most often, Cristiano would introduce a new concept and Mary would struggle with it for a few minutes. She would then revert back to an easier task that she already mastered, such as playing "Yankee Doodle." And, given Cristiano's keen understanding of Mary's condition, he would let her play out her diversion and then gradually look for ways to get back to the new concept. Within a few weeks or months, the new concept would be mastered and they moved on to the next thing.

Though we rarely had a session where Mary took a huge leap forward, we continued to see progress little by little. Those two sessions per week, completed week after week after week, really added up in terms of Mary's experience at the piano and her skill development. In fact, after one year with Cristiano, Mary learned to play "Jingle Bells" with both hands. The same girl who once couldn't sit still on a piano bench for five minutes, who spent more time studying Cristiano's glasses than the piano keys, who needed handfuls of Skittles to cooperate, was able and happy to sit and read the "Jingle Bells" sheet music and play with both hands simultaneously!

In fact, Mary now performs her favorite songs for family and friends. "Yankee Doodle," "Jingle Bells" and "Mary Had a Little Lamb" are clearly her favorites, and she is able to play other short songs as well. The satisfaction I feel seeing Mary sit at the piano, read music and play an entire song is hard to put into words. It's even more exciting to watch her play a full song and then turn around and soak in the applause. Her huge grins and appreciation of the attention are light years away from where she was just a few years ago.

We continued to see Cristiano every week until just before Mary's eighth birthday, at which point Cristiano got married and took a full-time job as a music teacher at a high school in Manhattan. We were very sorry to part ways with Cristiano, but we had nothing but thanks and praise for his work. Mary now plays piano on a weekly basis, working with an enthusiastic young man named Michael. Mary adjusted quickly to Michael's teaching and the transition from Cristiano to Michael went better than we ever could have expected. Michael has three young children of his own so his patience level with Mary has been fantastic and he's learned to adapt to her learning style while pushing forward with more discipline in other areas such as posture and following the correct beat.

The secret beneficiary of all those lessons is me. I always admired piano music and wanted to learn to play. However, it wasn't until we started going to Cristiano that I actually started learning. In helping the kids practice at home, I kept pace with their development and now I can read sheet music and play simple songs. It's a joy to sit around the living room now and all of us, including Marty, can chip in with some piano music.

18. Finishing Kindergarten, Sort Of

By the spring of 2007, we were pretty sure that Mary was not going to get a strong endorsement for first grade from the school. In fact, with Mary's out-of-seat behavior still an issue and with her reluctance to demonstrate her capabilities to her teachers on a regular basis, we were beginning to wonder if her spot in the ASD Nest Program was in jeopardy. Mary's teachers and classmates adored her because of her warmth and her hugs and her easy-going nature. However, the teachers were frustrated by her lack of focus and inability to complete non-preferred tasks.

Debby and I talked about the possibility of having Mary repeat Kindergarten. With her late September birthday, she was one of the youngest kids in her class, putting her at a slight disadvantage. (Two of the autistic kids in her class had January birthdays, meaning they were nearly nine months older than Mary.) We talked to several family members, including my brother-in-law Dennis in California and Debby's Uncle Charley in Illinois, both of whom have great experience as public school teachers, principals and administrators. Both Dennis and Charley stressed that repeating a grade would be easiest at a younger age, with Kindergarten the ideal grade to repeat if necessary.

As we talked to family members and analyzed the situation, our focus began to shift. We no longer thought about fighting the idea of holding Mary back and instead started seeing positives for her in repeating Kindergarten. By repeating, Mary would be one of the older students in class instead of the youngest. She would also have another full year to improve her verbal and communication skills. And, instead of barely keeping up with the curriculum, she would be reviewing a lot of the material and potentially getting slightly ahead.

However, we knew that Mary's spot in the ASD Nest Program was a blessing and we didn't want to give that up. We weren't sure the extent to which the school district was really aware of Mary's challenges in class, but we were pretty sure they had a good idea because the teachers, principal, therapists and school district representatives met regularly to discuss the program and monitor developments. Nevertheless, we were hesitant to discuss our concerns with anyone besides her teachers for fear that she might get kicked out of the program. We didn't know if repeating Kindergarten automatically bumped Mary from the program, so we avoided the subject. Turns out, the district leadership was well aware of Mary's positives and negatives and was spending plenty of time thinking about what to do with her and others like Mary.

One of the top special education administrators in Queens personally reviewed Mary's case. She felt there had to be a place for someone like Mary. She already knew that Mary's IQ was tested as normal, and she had had discussions with Mary's teachers so she knew that Mary had mastered many aspects of the Kindergarten curriculum. But Mary's inability to complete certain tasks and focus as required was troubling enough that she couldn't move on to first grade within the ASD Nest program. Everyone felt that Mary required too much attention and was a distraction to other students in the class. In addition, the first-grade Nest classes contain up to 16 students, an increase in class size that likely would not serve Mary well at that point.

To our amazement, the district administration worked out a one-time deal so that Mary could attend an intensive, repeat Kindergarten class at another nearby school. Though temporarily out of the existing ASD Nest Program, Mary would remain squarely on the ASD Nest team's radar by spending a year in a small class setting with three other ASD students. The Intensive-K class, as it became called, was set up as an off-shoot of the existing ASD Nest Program to give extra help to higher-functioning autistic children to master the basic Kindergarten skills of following instructions, staying in seats, walking quietly in the hallways, etc. The teacher received specific training to work with autistic children. Two teaching aids were assigned to the classroom at all times, as well as another teacher shared between two classes. In addition, the children were to receive speech therapy daily and occupational therapy as mandated in their IEPs.

Such a class setting did not previously exist within the NYC school district we were told. We were also told repeatedly that this was a one-year deal. There would be no intensive first-grade setting the following year, so the kids had to do well to get placed the following year in the most appropriate first-grade setting, whatever that may be.

For us, this was an unheard of level of attention and services. We cannot stress enough how appreciative we were and are to everyone in the school district who helped put together this program. These amazing people really wanted four young children to succeed. Our biggest concern when we accepted Mary's spot in the Intensive-K program was not how Mary would do in her repeat Kindergarten year but how would she handle the transition out of this four-person class setting back into a larger, first-grade setting. But that was a worry for another day and year; we knew Mary was going to get an incredible education in her repeat Kindergarten year and we readily accepted it.

Mary just had to finish out the last few weeks of school and enjoy the summer. Back in her ASD Nest Kindergarten program, the children were preparing for an end-of-the-year musical concert. Each grade was to sing several songs, with introductions from various children. Belinda was selected as one of the children to help welcome the parents and family members. Because Mary and Belinda had become friends, and Mary wanted to go wherever Belinda went, Mary followed Belinda onto the stage when they were rehearsing the introductory portion of the show. Mary's teachers quickly realized that Mary would enjoy following Belinda to the microphone, so they gave Mary a speaking line during the introduction! We found out about this only a few days before the show and were simultaneously amazed, nervous and excited.

For so long Mary wouldn't talk to anyone, respond to anyone or even be in the same room with her own parents. Now she was going up on stage in front of hundreds of strangers to speak into the microphone? Was that really possible? It was indeed possible. We arrived early on the night of the show and found seats in the middle of the auditorium. Very quickly the auditorium filled up. It was crowded and somewhat noisy. Right on schedule, the classes came out one by one and took their places on the bleachers set up on stage. Debby and I immediately noticed that nobody held Mary's hand or shoulder as they walked in and took their places, a noted improvement from her pre-Kindergarten graduation ceremony a year earlier.

Then, right on cue, six young children walked down from the bleachers and formed a line behind the microphone. Each child had a small part in the introduction. And yes, Mary was one of those children. She walked right down and took her place behind Belinda. Each child said his or her small part, then returned to the bleachers. Mary waited patiently as the other five children spoke their parts and then departed. Finally, Mary walked right up to the microphone, leaned in close and said clearly "We hope you enjoy the show!" She then quickly walked right back up to her spot in the bleachers and started singing the first song with the rest of her class. Debby and I nearly lost it, we were so choked up. In fact, we both were teary eyed for a few minutes. I know that in fifty years I will still recall that very moment and the sheer joy and encouragement I felt in seeing Mary successfully welcome everyone to that show.

In the interest of full disclosure, I have to say that Mary later bolted from her spot on the bleachers and introduced an upcoming song, a role that was supposed to be performed by one of the other children. So even on her night of glory, Mary reminded us (and everyone in the auditorium) that there was plenty of work still to be done in her recovery. But, as I pointed out to Debby, Mary did introduce that other song correctly, it just wasn't her responsibility to do it.

The end of the school year coincided with the timing of the Autism Speaks "Walk Now for Autism" event in New York City. Debby and I formed a team and raised over $5,000 for Autism Speaks, a wonderful organization that works to promote autism awareness and fundraising for autism research. The walk was held in lower Manhattan in Battery Park along the waterfront.

We designed a tee-shirt with our team name on the front: Something About Mary. On the back it showed the date as well as a stick-figure drawing Mary made of a person walking. Our team wore the shirts as we completed the two-mile walk along the Hudson River. Joining us on the walk were Mary's speech teacher and her family. The speech teacher was one of Mary's biggest fans at school that year and really did a lot to help Mary progress in her speech and social interactions.

Other than temporarily losing Charlie in the post-walk chaos, which was a five-minute panic for all of us, the day was a tremendous success. We saw many families walking together to promote autism awareness and saw so many people volunteering and making a difference. It was truly heartwarming to see thousands of people rallying for a cause, a cause that is finally starting to get national attention and increased funding for research.

For years autism research lagged far behind other childhood disorders in terms of research funding, but that is starting to change thanks to the efforts of people at Autism Speaks and other important organizations. There are "Walk Now for Autism" events all over the country, all raising money for autism research. Each walk is also an opportunity to see just how many people are affected by autism. It is truly heart wrenching.

The autism walks are also motivating and illuminating, and that was underscored by our young nephew Rory. During the 2007 walk in Manhattan, Rory, who was 6 at the time, proudly wore his Something About Mary team tee-shirt and trudged along with the rest of us. A week later, we visited his family and Rory was wearing his Something About Mary shirt once again. He told Debby he enjoyed the autism walk and that he loved helping Mary. He continued, saying he wanted to do the walk every year if he could because he knows Mary has autism and wants to help her. It is often said that kids can be so mean and cruel, but we know that many kids can also be sweet, caring and sympathetic. It was a pleasure to hear Rory talk that way about Mary.

With the successful walk behind us, our thoughts turned to the summer break. We knew Mary would be receiving plenty of help in the intensive Kindergarten program in the fall but before we reached that point, we hoped to see improvement in other areas over the summer.

19. The Gluten-Free, Casein-Free Diet

As we said goodbye to Castlewood Elementary and the regular ASD Nest Program, we prepared for a summer of adventure and challenges. The first challenge, in fact was already beginning. On June 1 we decided to put Mary on a gluten-free and casein-free diet.[12] For two solid years, we had been focusing on Mary's behavioral therapy and not paying much attention to her diet. Like many other parents of autistic kids, we had read about the gluten-free diet but never tried it because Mary never had shown any obvious outward allergic reactions to gluten or casein. In fact, we had Mary tested by an allergist who found no allergic reactions to wheat, gluten or milk and dairy products.

Gluten and casein are proteins – gluten is found primarily in wheat, barley, rye and oat products and casein primarily in milk and dairy products. Anecdotal evidence is piling up that shows kids on the autism spectrum often show marked improvement in a variety of ways when put on a strict, gluten-free, casein-free (GFCF) diet for at least three months. Among other things, autistic kids reportedly sleep better, become less "spacey" and have drastically improved bowel functions when following a GFCF diet.

There has been widespread disagreement over the effectiveness of a GFCF diet. As of the writing of this book, no scientific study had yet proven that a GFCF diet effectively lessens the symptoms of autism. Joining the science skeptics were nutritionists concerned about the potential shortcomings of a GFCF diet. Children get calcium and Vitamin D from milk and fiber from breads and cereals. Avoiding these items can be unhealthy unless the parents closely monitor what their child eats and drinks and finds appropriate substitutions. Additionally, we have heard and seen a few educators who dismiss the GFCF diet as nonsense, instead preaching the virtues of behavioral therapy and proven educational strategies. For these very reasons, and for the undeniable challenge of sticking to a GFCF diet, we never gave it a try for two full years after Mary's autism diagnosis.

Mary's speech therapist at Castlewood casually asked us after school one day near the end of the school year if we were concerned about Mary's diet. We said yes, we were concerned because she was a picky eater and we thought she should eat healthier. At that point, she recommended the book *Healing the New Childhood Epidemics: Autism, ADHD, Asthma and Allergies* by Kenneth Bock, M.D. and Cameron Stauth.[13] The authors talk in great detail about the relationship between diet and physical-chemical imbalances and the impact they have on the behavior of children suffering from autism, asthma, allergies and attention-deficit/hyperactivity disorder.

Mary's speech therapist said she noticed that Mary often turned her head and looked at people and objects out of the extreme corner of her eye. She had read that such behavior was common in autistic children who were lacking in Vitamin A. The therapist, recognizing that her role did not really include making dietary recommendations to parents, made sure she told us about her observation after school hours and with apologies for potentially stepping beyond her role. There was a comfort level between us and Mary's speech therapist that had developed over the course of the year and we respected the therapist and took her recommendation as a friendly gesture.

The book was an eye-opener for us immediately and we are forever grateful to Mary's speech therapist for her recommendation. Among many other things, the book described a condition often called "leaky gut syndrome," in which the digestive systems of some children do not process foods correctly, leading to a leaking gut which sends proteins into the bloodstream. To simplify a complicated theory, this process then causes proteins to reach the brain and have an opiate-like effect on kids. That is why many kids become so addicted to foods like chicken nuggets, pizza and macaroni and cheese. They literally crave these foods, which their bodies don't process properly, then the proteins enter the bloodstream and work like opiates on their brains. This causes many children, the theory goes, to become spacey and disengaged, although often in a very happy state of mind.

In so many ways the Bock book just made a lot of sense. We recalled that Mary's teachers would often comment on Mary taking a long time in the bathroom. They would also comment from time to time that Mary was passing gas in class. The bathroom difficulties and flatulation had gotten to the point that Debby had taken Mary to a children's hospital to see a specialist. Debby mentioned the Bock book and the possibility of a leaky gut. That doctor tested Mary for Celiac disease, a condition in which gluten is not tolerated by the body, but Mary tested negative for that disorder. The specialist did not believe in the "leaky gut syndrome" that Dr. Bock wrote about in his book and dismissed the idea entirely. In fact, the doctor did not suggest any dietary changes for Mary whatsoever.

It was our good luck that the book's primary author worked at a health clinic only two hours from our house, so we decided to make an appointment to visit the health center as soon as possible. Unfortunately, due to the book's growing popularity we had to wait two months for an appointment. We eagerly took the late August appointment and then got started right away on the book's first suggestion: moving to a gluten-free and casein-free diet for at least three months. If the diet didn't help, Mary could just go back to the old diet. However, if the diet led to improved behavior, then Mary would benefit.

As we prepared for the big change in Mary's diet, we learned that many people, adults and children alike, have allergic *sensitivities* to gluten and casein even though they don't demonstrate obvious outward allergic *reactions* to them. Was that the case with Mary? We were determined to find out, even if it meant dramatically altering the way we ate and shopped and lived our lives. We would try it out over the summer and hope for the best.

It was a daunting challenge to be sure. Gluten is everywhere. It's in bread and cereal and pizza crust and cookies and oatmeal and crackers and pretzels and hot dogs and ketchup and flour tortillas and even the breading on the outside of chicken nuggets. And casein is in milk and ice cream and butter and cheese and many other common foods.

The new diet meant no more of Mary's favorite cereals for breakfast, no more grilled cheese sandwiches at lunch and no more pizza or macaroni and cheese for dinner. Our family tradition of ordering cheese pizzas every Friday night, which started during the Catholic celebration of Lent a few years before when we couldn't eat meat on Fridays, became a thing of the past. The new diet also meant no more trips to the ice cream store, which even during Mary's darkest days of regression was always a happy place for the family. It meant no more milk with dinner and no more eating out at the mall or restaurants without seriously thinking about what we were ordering.

Fortunately, there is a large and growing industry that caters to those seeking to avoid gluten and casein. Though the products are generally more expensive than their mass marketed gluten-laden counterparts, there are gluten-free cookies and pretzels and pastas available. And there are rice milk and vegan cheese substitutes. Also, a growing number of pizzerias are offering gluten-free pizza crusts, including one place just 10 minutes from our home in Queens. Mary used to pick the cheese off pizza anyway, so now we order gluten-free pizza with no cheese and she loves it. From a nutrition standpoint, we find the best options usually are just going with meats and fruits and vegetables and avoiding most boxed or canned products.

We immediately eliminated gluten products from our cupboards and casein products from our refrigerator, with a few exceptions for Dad, Charlie and Marty. Debby decided to join Mary on the gluten-free and casein-free diet as a show of support. Because it was the beginning of summer, we started grilling chicken and steak more frequently. At first they rebelled against grilled chicken and demanded chicken nuggets, but we held firm and they took to eating grilled chicken fairly quickly. We tried four or five different soy milk options, with limited success, but then found a rice milk that Mary liked and was perfectly happy to drink. It was available at the local grocery store, came in a carton just like the other milk, and we bought the enriched kind that has extra calcium and Vitamin D that Mary needs. We found several gluten-free cereals that she could eat in the mornings, and we bought gluten-free pancake mix and make pancakes most weekends. Eggs were OK, so Mary had hard-boiled eggs for lunch several times per week.

The following are some examples of what Mary eats in place of her old diet:

- Breakfast:
  - Scrambled eggs with avocado and corn tortillas
  - Hard-boiled eggs
  - Gluten-free cereal with rice milk
  - Gluten-free pancakes (add applesauce for extra flavor and moisture)
  - Gluten-free pasta with olive oil

- Lunch:
  - Quesadillas made with vegan cheese and corn tortillas
  - Gluten-free pasta
  - Hard boiled eggs
  - Gluten-free hot dogs, sliced with no bun; French fries
  - Cheese sandwich made with vegan cheese and gluten-free bread
  - Carrot sticks
  - Apple slices

- Snack:
  - Fruit, especially apples
  - Carrot sticks
  - Popcorn, salted but no butter
  - Corn chips or tortilla chips
  - Gluten-free pretzels
  - Raisins

- Dinner:
  - Steak with rice or potatoes and steamed vegetable
  - Grilled chicken with rice or potatoes and steamed vegetable
  - Steamed vegetables (mostly broccoli, corn, green beans or carrots)
  - Gluten-free hot dogs, sliced with no bun; French fries
  - Gluten-free pizza
  - Gluten-free pasta with meatballs
  - Quesadillas with vegan cheese and corn tortillas
  - Chili with tortilla chips and avocado

- Desserts:
  - Ice pops
  - Frozen ices
  - Gluten-free cookies or gluten-free cupcakes
  - Watermelon

Though the diet caused us much stress and anguish at first, we embraced it completely and began to reap immediate benefits. Within a week of starting the diet, Mary started sleeping through the night every night. Night wakings were gone! That alone was worth continuing the diet, even if nothing else changed. Not having Mary wake up for hours at a time during the night was a huge win for the whole family. From what we read, the night wakings were probably caused by indigestion, since Mary's body was not able to process the gluten correctly. Once awakened, Mary's echolalia would kick in and that, along with the stomach queasiness, would keep her awake for hours.

We also noticed that Mary's flatulating was occurring less and less often. She went from passing gas every hour to going days without passing any gas at all. Also, in the past Mary would often pull up her shirt and grab her belly with both hands, kind of balling up the fatty flab around her belly button and squeezing it. I always thought she was just playing around, but I came to realize that she actually was having discomfort in her belly and squeezing it relieved the nausea to a degree. Because Mary's communication skills were so lacking, she didn't tell us that her stomach hurt, she just kept eating her favorite foods then passing gas, squeezing her stomach and waking up at all hours of the night. When the new diet started to take hold, we noticed Mary rarely grabbed her stomach flab anymore, although for many months she still had a somewhat swollen belly for an otherwise healthy and thin kid. There have been occasional minor lapses in the diet, but usually those occur away from home when we fail to plan ahead and have less control over what Mary eats.

I strongly recommend the GFCF diet. Despite the lack of scientific evidence that a GFCF diet lessens the symptoms of autism, the anecdotal evidence from families such as ours that have tried the diet has been overwhelming. The diet usually works to some degree, and in many cases has had dramatic and life-changing success. Autism Speaks, one of the largest autism-related organizations in the United States and the world, mentions the GFCF diet on its web site but as of this writing it neither encourages nor discourages the diet. The site mentions that many families find it helpful, but also points out the lack of scientific evidence thus far and emphasizes the need for nutritional substitutes.

As far as I'm concerned, raising an autistic child while relying only on behavioral therapy alone, without trying a gluten-free, casein-free diet, is like driving a car with the emergency brake engaged. You can drive the car forward, but it requires tremendous effort to make just a little progress. Release that emergency brake though and the car zooms forward. The same may be true for many children with autism, where the gluten and casein they ingest act like emergency brakes, drastically slowing the pace of progress. Teachers, parents and therapists work hard and give tremendous effort but their efforts may be undermined by those proteins swirling about inside the child, causing him or her to space out and lose focus. However, eliminate the gluten and casein and watch the child take off! Though reportedly the diet may not work for everyone, it's absolutely worth a try. It can't hurt to try the diet for three months, honestly sticking to the diet for 90 days and not cheating. I do recommend consulting a pediatrician or nutritionist during the diet trial to ensure all the child's nutritional needs are met. If it doesn't work, you haven't lost much, but if it does work and leads to rapid progress, then the GFCF diet will just become a way of life.

20. Disney World a Delight

Mary's diet was our immediate concern once the school year ended. We went on a family trip to Disney World in Florida the last week of June, and we were dreading the dietary restrictions for weeks. We knew Mary would be surrounded by gluten-laden temptations inside the park as well as when we got together in the evenings with her cousins, aunts and uncles who were joining us on the trip. In addition, we knew Mary didn't like crowded and noisy situations, something she would be surrounded with at Disney World.

Our anxiety turned out to be for naught though. Prior to leaving for Florida, we stopped at our pediatrician's office and asked the doctor to write a short letter stating that Mary has autism and that any special accommodations that Disney could make for Mary would be helpful. I read this tip online at some point while we were planning our vacation and decided to give it a try. Sure enough, the staff at Disney World was amazing and made sure we had an incredible vacation to remember.

The first day when we entered the Magic Kingdom, we went to the guest relations center and gave them the letter from Mary's pediatrician. The Disney employees were courteous and respectful. They didn't challenge the authenticity of the note or look at Mary skeptically. Instead, they gave us special passes and told us to show them to the employees at each attraction and that we would be given special considerations. For some rides, we were told to go to the top of the exit ramp and we would be allowed to get on the next ride. For other rides, we were allowed to bypass the long lines and just enter the shorter line where people had picked up Fast Pass tickets earlier in the day. In effect, we had the equivalent of a Fast Pass for every ride in the park.

I felt guilty the first few times we used the passes, but I quickly realized that Mary did not have the capacity to wait in long lines in the 98-degree heat. When we did decide to wait in line, it was a nightmare. The line to get a photo and autograph and to see Mickey Mouse was supposedly only 20-30 minutes long, so we decided to just wait and not use our passes. Unfortunately, after 20 minutes we were nowhere near the front of the line and Mary was getting anxious and wouldn't sit or stand still. At that point we decided to go back to the employee at the front of the autograph tent and we showed him our passes. Without hesitation, he brought us around a back entrance and let us go in with the next group in line. We probably saved 45 minutes and more importantly, we prevented a Mary meltdown and she got to see Mickey Mouse up close. We then got to see Daisy Duck and Minnie Mouse as well and the kids were all thrilled.

During the entire stay at Disney World, not one customer ever complained about our special-needs pass or gave us a dirty look. We have found that with autism, especially Mary's rather high-functioning form of autism, strangers look at Mary's face and cannot see her disability. It is a disability that shows itself in Mary's actions and lack of social awareness. So for us to bring a "normal" looking daughter to the park and receive such first-class treatment without any funny looks or challenges from anyone was truly wonderful.

We stayed at a time-share property near the park. Our two-bedroom suite featured a full kitchen stocked with pots and pans and dishes and utensils. We started the trip with a visit to the local grocery store and stocked up on healthy foods and had breakfast and dinner every day at the time-share. We controlled most of Mary's eating by avoiding park food. Then, to our surprise, we were able to find several decent food options within the park so Mary was able to completely enjoy herself and still stick to her new special diet.

A few weeks after returning home from Disney World, we were emboldened by Mary's success with the diet and decided to try sending her to summer camp for a week with Charlie. A nearby program, called FasTracKids, offered children ages 4-10 a half day learning environment. Children arrived at 9 a.m. and stayed until noon. Then they were done for the day and went home. A different subject was covered each week, such as astronomy or magic or geography. The subjects were somewhat academic and challenging for the kids, but at the same time the children had a lot of fun with it.

Charlie had attended FasTracKids for the first part of the summer and loved it. Mary, meanwhile, attended a summer-school program through the school district. There was a one-week gap between the end of Mary's program and the end of the FasTracKids program. We decided that rather than have Mary sit around the house all week while I worked upstairs, we would send her to camp with Charlie. We were honest with the center director and told her we had some concerns about Mary's ability to stay seated. However, we told her that Mary was bright and loving and that Charlie would help keep her in line.

As an aside, by that point I had unofficially deputized Charlie to be his sister's keeper. Charlie has always been a wonderful kid and a bright student. Things came easy to him, so I knew he would do well at FasTracKids. And by that point he had several weeks of experience at camp, so I asked him to help keep Mary in her seat if possible and to coach her on how to behave if she started to act up.

In fact, Charlie's deputy role had been emerging for more than a year, somewhat by necessity and somewhat by his own choosing. With Debby at work all day and with baby Marty requiring so much attention, I didn't always have the ability to literally hold Mary's hand and guide her through every situation. So I started asking Charlie to help Mary when dealing with simple things.

Back at FasTracKids, I dropped the kids off at 8:30 a.m. and then took Marty to the babysitter before I went to work. I figured I had a good three hours of solid work time. Wrong—the phone rang at 9:15 a.m. It was the camp director asking me to come and get Mary. She had seen a computer in the corner that they use to project items onto the big board in the front of the room and all Mary wanted to do was to use that computer to play games. (They tried several times to talk her into sitting in her seat and to get her to cooperate with the class, to no avail.) When I got there, everyone was very apologetic and sympathetic but they just couldn't allow Mary to stay and disrupt the class. I agreed of course, and took Mary home. I squeezed her hand and kissed her on top of the head and said, "Let's go home."

Days like those are difficult and remind you that the journey is on-going. Mary wasn't ready for that environment yet and that was that. I also felt bad for Charlie, because he was old enough to realize that Mary was not behaving right and he probably felt embarrassed at his sister's antics. To his credit, Charlie didn't make fun of Mary (at least not in front of me) and he never complained about Mary's bad day at camp.

We spent the rest of the summer playing at the various parks nearby, swimming at a nearby lake and teaching Mary and Charlie to read. I bought a book called *Teach Your Child to Read in 100 Easy Lessons* by Siegfried Engelmann, Phyllis Haddox and Elaine Brruner,[14] and decided that we would get through those 100 lessons before the kids went back to school. I hoped to solidify Mary's reading skills and give Charlie a head start on his pre-Kindergarten peers. The kids did an excellent job following along with the lessons and we reached lesson 78 by the end of August. At that point, the lessons were considerably longer than the early lessons, often taking 20 minutes apiece to get through. By then though, they were both sounding out words and recognizing common letter grouping, such as CH and TH and SH. Both could read basic Level 1 books by the time summer ended so we were pleased with that.

As the end of August neared, we prepared for major changes. Marty was cruising around the house and walking would be only weeks away. Charlie was about to start full-day pre-Kindergarten at the big elementary school two blocks away. Mary meanwhile was to attend her third school in three years, repeating Kindergarten in her intensive-K program. But first, it was finally time to visit Dr. Bock's health center in upstate New York.

21. Starting the Biomedical Program

We dropped off Marty and Charlie at Debby's sister Rachel's house and made the drive upstate on August 31, 2007, unsure of what the future would hold for us and for Mary. Our destination was the health clinic in Rhinebeck, New York, a small town approximately two hours north of New York City. Mary's new diet was working out great and we were eager to take Mary's therapy to a new level.

Dr. Bock's book, which I referred to earlier is filled with anecdotes about patients treated at the Rhinebeck Health Center over the past decade, many of whom made unbelievable progress. Kids who weren't previously talking now walked in and had conversations with the doctors and nurses. Youngsters who had bowel problems and major stomach problems were potty trained and lived normal lives. Children who had isolated themselves in their own little worlds were now interacting in a meaningful way with the people around them.

We so wanted Mary to be the next success story. We didn't see any reason why she couldn't. We knew the potential was there inside of Mary, because we had seen all of her happiness and enthusiasm and interactions as a 1- and 2-year old. We wanted the doctors to help lead Mary the rest of the way out of the darkness and into a more meaningful life with us. We wanted that bright and sunny 2-year old to come back to us, and we believed that a biomedical approach might be the missing ingredient in Mary's therapy.

Dr. Bock and his team in Rhinebeck believe that the cause of autism is not primarily genetic but is a combination of genetics and the environment. One of Dr. Bock's often quoted lines from the *Healing the New Childhood Epidemics* book is "Genetics, so to speak, load the gun, and environment pulls the trigger." I highly recommend reading Dr. Bock's book for a more detailed explanation of what he sees as the causes of autism as well as the myriad of ways to treat the condition. I am not qualified to go into that level of detail, and that goes beyond the scope of this book. But I will say that Debby and I liked what we read in Dr. Bock's book and that his healing program seemed to make a lot of sense to us. We were ready and willing to work with the doctors in Rhinebeck to see what more could be done for Mary.

The success of Dr. Bock's books we were told, along with his track record of successful treatments, made him a much-sought after individual, so he often travels to attend conferences and seminars, appears on television programs, etc. Thus, he had an incredibly long waiting list for new patients. Debby and I decided to see one of Dr. Bock's co-workers, Dr. Michael Compain, instead. Even then, as I mentioned previously, there was a three-month waiting period.

The road to Rhinebeck is lovely, very rural and open. It's a nice break from the congestion of New York City. Debby, Mary and I pulled up in front of the medical center right on time and got out of the car. We expected to see a gleaming, shiny medical complex, something truly state of the art and revolutionary to go along with the forward-minded thinking that was going on in the center. In fact, the building is a converted old Victorian house built over 100 years ago! I smiled at the irony, knowing there are fancy medical offices all over the U.S. full of intelligent doctors who are following traditional medical practices and making little or no progress when treating autistic children. Then here's an old house in the middle of rural America where truly innovative and ground-breaking work is being done and lives are literally being transformed on a regular basis.

Inside we met Dr. Compain and we began the next phase of our journey. Dr. Compain, like Dr. Bock, is often referred to as a DAN! Doctor because he believes autism is a medical disorder that can be treated by focusing on the root causes of autism. The term DAN! Doctor comes from the Autism Research Institute and its Defeat Autism Now! project. According to its website, the Autism Research Institute[15] has been "convening recurring meetings for carefully selected physicians, researchers and scientists committed to finding effective treatments for autism" since 1995. While Debby and I had no affiliation with the Defeat Autism Now! project or the Autism Research Institute, as parents of an autistic child we felt an obligation to explore the biomedical options to see if we could further accelerate Mary's recovery through these treatment strategies.

After an initial physical examination, Dr. Mike (as everyone there seems to call him) sat with us and listened as we explained Mary's rise, regression and challenges. He listened and listened and listened for nearly an hour!

Dr. Mike had an easy-going personality and a wonderful demeanor. He wore the typical doctor's white lab coat with a stethoscope around his neck. He had large understanding eyes that seemed to simultaneously observe everything Mary was doing while also recognizing Debby and I as we spoke to him. Throughout our discussion, Dr. Mike sat with perfect posture in his backless chair, took notes and asked relevant questions, then said he thought there was a good chance he could help Mary.

He explained that every child is different and thus every treatment program is different. Further, the degree of improvement varied by individual, too, and all we could do was hope for the best with Mary. Based on successful programs they had completed before, they had a pretty good idea of what would work with her. Nevertheless it would be a trial-and-error program, based on knowledge acquired from years of treatments, but remaining flexible based on Mary's actual results. Following the program would be a leap of faith on our part, but we knew that we didn't want Mary to continue plodding along as she was, so if Dr. Mike had suggestions we were going to listen.

The first thing Dr. Mike asked was that we have Mary take some blood tests. He wanted to see what deficiencies she had, if any, so we could treat those. He was glad to hear that Mary was already on the gluten-free, casein-free diet and that progress was being made there. We would meet again two months later to review Mary's blood tests and map out her healing program. In the meantime, he prescribed Vitamin B-12 shots. These were to be given every third day just above Mary's buttocks on her belt line. Dr. Mike explained that vitamin B-12 helps the body detoxify heavy metals, an environmental monkey wrench thrown into Mary's system.

At first I was concerned about having to give Mary a shot every third day. Like most kids I suppose, Mary did not particularly like getting shots from her doctor. How was I going to pull off this feat every third day? Surprisingly, Mary showed little anxiety over the B-12 injections. The needles were very short and administering the shot went quickly. I purchased a bright red "sharps" container at the nearby pharmacy, and each time I gave Mary an injection I put the used needle into the container. Within a week or two, every time Mary saw the sharps container she pulled up her shirt in the back and said "time for my shot" or something similar. She just kind of shrugged her shoulders as if to say let's get this done and move on!

After many months of getting the B12 shots with little or no reaction, one day Mary looked at me suspiciously as I approached with the needle and sharps container.

"Are you a doctor?" she finally asked curiously.

I had to laugh out loud on that one.

"No, I'm not a doctor," I reminded her. "But dads can give shots too if it helps their kids get better."

When we returned in October, Dr. Mike reviewed Mary's blood tests and noted several deficiencies and several areas where she had a heavy metal burden. Most of the program at that point would involve over-the-counter supplements, such as a multi-vitamin, vitamin B-6, methylfolate, pyridoxal-5-phosphate, cod liver oil with omega-3 and probiotics to help promote good digestion. She would also continue the vitamin B-12 shots and do a two-week trial aimed at clearing out any yeast overgrowth in her gut. To control the yeast, we were given a prescription for Diflucan, an antifungal.

Though the cost of all the supplements and the prescription was several hundred dollars, we knew that it was a drop in the bucket compared to the cost of most behavioral therapists. We were anxious to get going. Once we got home and put all of those supplement bottles in the cabinet, we realized we had a pretty daunting task at hand. Remembering to give Mary her supplements every day was the first challenge, then getting her to take them was the next. Fortunately, all of the supplements were in capsule form, so we could pull the casing apart and drop the powder into her orange juice in the morning and in her rice milk each evening. It was tiring at first though, as we felt like the pill police, always running after Mary with a supplement.

All of the supplements seemed to be having some impact. Mary's once-bulging stomach was flattening out to a more normal and healthy appearance and she was starting to talk to us a little more. We weren't having conversations, but Mary was responding to questions more frequently. Mary also seemed less sensitive to noise. For the first time in years, she consented to wearing regular blue jeans, as her sense of touch apparently was more tolerant now and the denim material no longer bothered her. At school, her teachers noted that Mary was able to stay on task longer and was not getting out of her seat much anymore. It was obvious to us that Mary was on the right track.

We returned to Rhinebeck again in December, just after Christmas, for our third visit and Dr. Mike asked how things were going. It had been four months since our first visit and Mary was getting used to all of the supplements. We explained that we were seeing some improvements and were happy with the progress so far, ready to keep moving forward. At that point Dr. Mike noted that he had high hopes for Mary based on her track record, that is, children who start off apparently "normal" then regress often respond well to the treatment program.

To paraphrase and summarize, Dr. Mike suggested that Mary probably suffered an inflammation in her brain as a 2-year old. This was likely caused by a weak immune system (genetics) and environmental factors (gluten and casein sensitivities, heavy metal toxins, immunizations, etc.). The problem was compounded for two to three years by Mary's diet. Thus, he believed that Mary's brain was not functioning optimally due to the inflammation, and this was exacerbated by the spaciness she felt and demonstrated prior to starting the gluten-free, casein-free diet.

Going forward, Dr. Mike said we would focus on relieving the brain inflammation and reducing the toxins in Mary's system. This sounded a bit scary to us, but we knew we would do so using FDA-approved prescriptions and supplements. We also prayed every day that we were doing the right thing for Mary and that she would soon emerge from her autistic world and connect in a more meaningful way with her family again. So, Mary started an anti-viral prescription (Zovirax) that winter for a six-month period. She also started taking trimethylglycine (TMG), which would help further with the methylation process of removing toxic metals from her body.

Dr. Mike said to especially watch the TMG, because many autistic kids respond quickly and powerfully to it. Specifically, an increase in language is often noted when kids start taking TMG. Sure enough, within days Mary was more talkative. She still wasn't having full blown conversations, but she started asking to go places and to visit people and relatives without being prompted. Though she wouldn't provide lengthy answers, we found that we could now sit with Mary and ask as many as four or five questions in a row and she would answer each of them appropriately. This was a huge improvement for her and we were delighted!

At our meeting in the late spring of 2008, Dr. Mike recommended that Mary try a medicated nasal spray called Oxytocin. He explained that during birth, a woman experiences a surge in the Oxytocin hormone that helps her to emotionally bond with her newborn baby. DAN! doctors have had success supplementing autistic children with Oxytocin to increase the children's emotional bonding with others.

Though I initially thought this was a bit of a stretch, Debby and I agreed to give it a try. The Oxytocin was introduced slowly, first in one nostril once a day, progressing to two nostrils twice a day. We found that Mary became more loving and interactive with all of us! On at least a half-dozen occasions within the first two months of using oxytocin, we observed Mary kissing her toddler brother Marty on the cheek, seemingly out of the blue. She also started saying, "I love you, Daddy," much more frequently, highlighted by one morning when, within a two-hour period, she hugged me three times and told me she loved me. Mary really began bonding with a young boy in her Kindergarten class as well, an astonishing improvement that I will discuss in more detail in Chapter 23.

We continue to see Dr. Mike every few months. We tweak Mary's supplements based on her improvements and the results Dr. Mike sees in her periodic blood tests. Each visit Dr. Mike reminds us that nutritional therapy is just one component of Mary's program, equally important are the behavioral and speech therapy that she receives. It is one thing to become more verbal; it is another to learn to speak and to interact appropriately with others. Fortunately for Mary, she was getting the behavioral and speech therapy she needed at school in her new Kindergarten program.

Note: The treatment program discussed in this chapter was devised by and closely monitored by a medical doctor based on direct observations and tests done on Mary. You should consult your physician before starting any new treatment program for yourself or your children. Mary's treatment program was discussed here for educational purposes only, to demonstrate the power of supplements and appropriate prescriptions in combating autism. The author has no affiliation with the Defeat Autism Now! organization or the Rhinebeck Health Center, except as a parent of a patient at the Rhinebeck Health Center.

22. Repeating Kindergarten Pays Off

Mary made the transition from Castlewood Elementary to Public School 165, also known as Bergtraum Elementary, with ease. The schools are in opposite directions from our house but each is a 10-minute drive away. As we had done the previous year, we took Mary to see her new school several times during the last week of August so she would get used to the drive and have a chance to see the school from the outside and play on the playground. By the time school started, Mary knew the school and never hesitated or complained about going there. For about a month, she asked to see her old teachers, but after awhile she seemed to move on mentally and, when asked about school, she mentioned her new teachers by name.

Debby and I never doubted our decision to hold Mary back for another year of Kindergarten, but it did feel awkward seeing neighbors and cousins Mary's age moving on to first grade. A small part of me felt like Mary was falling behind her peers, but in reality, she had fallen behind years ago. This was no time to focus on keeping up with peers; we had to focus on advancing Mary's skills and abilities.

The Intensive-K setting was exactly what Mary needed. The classroom wasn't huge, but it was a good sized room for a small class. In addition to Mary, there were three boys in the class: Ben (from Mary's first Kindergarten class the year before), Derrick and Tim (again not all their real names). All were on the higher functioning end of the autism spectrum and all needed to catch up academically and solidify their social and interpersonal skills. There were no typical students in the class as role models this time, just four spectrum kids.

One teacher led the class, with two aides and a swing teacher who also assisted in a second Intensive-K class composed of 5-year olds going through Kindergarten for first time. Both classes were well supported by the school principal. Mary's teacher was an energetic, young woman with long brown hair named Ms. Meredith (later Mrs. Greene after getting married the next summer). She proved to be just what the kids needed. She kept an aggressive academic curriculum, mixing in first-grade level reading comprehension activities to push the children past the traditional Kindergarten level work. We were told before the year began that some first-grade material would be added throughout the year, so the students weren't doing a complete Kindergarten do-over.

Mary started the year with limited reading skills. Her sight word vocabulary was close to 100 words, and she learned quite a bit over the summer working with me in the *Teach Your Child to Read in 100 Easy Lessons* book. But sounding out new words remained a challenge. Prior to the Christmas holiday break, parents were invited to join the class for an hour to see the children in class. On the day Debby and I were invited to observe, Mary worked with the speech therapist to sound out silly words. Instead of writing real words on the flip charts, the speech therapist, a tall, young woman with long dark hair, wrote nonsense words such as N-U-V and T-A-L. When the kids took turns reading the nonsense words, you could clearly hear them sounding out each letter. There was no way they had memorized the words already as sight words because they were not real words.

The speech therapist explained that at the beginning of the school year, they didn't use letters at all but instead had cards showing various gestures. These gestures included clapping hands, blowing a kiss, etc. The therapist would line up three cards and the kids learned to do each activity in sequence. Gradually, they started swapping out some of the gestures for letters, so the three cards might show a hand clapping, the letter P and a card showing blow a kiss. The students would clap, say the "P" sound and then blow a kiss. This progressed until the action cards were completely replaced by letters. The kids followed right along and began saying the three letter sounds.

Debby and I sat excitedly and listened as Mary sounded out a half dozen words correctly. The entire time she stayed in her seat and remained focused on the activity. Not once did she get up and walk around or cause the teachers any grief. That, in and of itself, was a huge accomplishment for Mary and a relief for us. We were growing more and more optimistic about Mary's future, and knew that she had to develop the ability to follow instructions and listen to teachers if she were ever really to move forward. To see her sit and wait her turn at school, then give the correct answers by reading and sounding out letters, was truly wonderful.

Mary's math skills also improved during the first few months of the new school year. She was adding and subtracting numbers by counting her fingers or other objects, such as green beans on her dinner plate. We'd play a game during dinner, using green beans or other food items. We'd ask Mary to count the items, then have her eat some or add some to her plate and count again. Mary not only responded to our requests but was able to give the right answers.

During the first part of the school year we decided to move to a bigger house down the street. While walking through the neighborhood the previous spring, we noticed a For Sale by Owner sign on a house with a much bigger yard than ours. While most yards in our neighborhood were 40x100 lots, this one had an irregular but large lot with 82 feet across in front, 45 feet across in back and a depth of 120 feet. The house had four bedrooms and two-and-a-half bathrooms, compared to the 3-bedroom and one-and-a-half bathroom home we were living in for the past seven years. It took several months to finally close on the house, and then we moved in October.

We were curious how well Mary would adapt to the new house, but it turned out to be a non-issue. By this time Mary was interactive with us enough that we could explain to her that we were moving and that the new house would be our home going forward. On the first night we stayed at the new house, Mary finished dinner then asked to go home. We reiterated that we were home and that if Mary was tired she could go upstairs to her same old bunk bed in her new bedroom. She did just that, fell right asleep and never mentioned the old house again! It was that easy.

As the months went by, Debby and I continued to receive regular updates from Mary's teachers about her progress. Much like the year before, the teachers and therapists at Mary's new school all really took a liking to her. There's something about Mary's happy demeanor and warmth that really touches people and Mary's magic was working again at her new school. As we saw Mary's reading improve and watched her handwriting get dramatically better, Debby and I knew that we had made the right decision about repeating Kindergarten. Rather than struggling to keep up, Mary was confidently completing assignments, staying with the group in class and focusing on the task at hand instead of drifting off into her own world at every opportunity.

In early January, the parents of the Intensive-K children were called to a meeting with the school principal, a social worker and several of the top regional special education administrators. It was announced at that time that a second ASD Nest Program would be formed in Queens, right there at Mary's school. The best-case intention was that the four children in the Intensive-K class would move on to first grade the following September as the first ASD Nest first grade class in the school. The current 5-year old Intensive-K class was to become the school's first ASD Nest Kindergarten class the following September as well, so that the school would begin the formal ASD Nest structure with Kindergarten and first grade classes while possibly continuing the turning-5 intensive Kindergarten class.

This news meant that if Mary continued to show progress and an ability to stay on task, she would be rejoining the standard ASD Nest Program and would not have to change schools again. She could stay at the same building and work with the same therapists, albeit potentially with a new teacher in the fall. Debby and I were, of course, ecstatic to hear this news. The alternatives to the ASD Nest Program were more restrictive, and we said prayers every chance we got that Mary would get back in the standard Nest Program. This would allow her to continue receiving therapy and working with teachers trained to work with autistic children. It also meant moving to a larger class size and learning alongside typical children, as she had done at Castlewood the previous year.

The only concern we had about rejoining the standard ASD Nest Program was the increase in class size. Going from the present four-student class to as many as 16 children scared us a little, because there was the chance that Mary would get much less individual attention and that she might start losing focus again. However, the benefits of the program were so great that we never considered taking Mary anywhere else. She would just have to keep improving and learning to complete tasks, and we would seek opportunities throughout the rest of the year for Mary to spend time each week integrating into a larger class.

When spring rolled around, Mary's interactions with peers had increased substantially. Mary's speech therapist took one day per month to focus on each child, recording every interaction the child had for an hour. The interactions were classified as With Peer, With Adult or With Herself. At the parent-teacher conference in late March, the speech therapist showed us a column graph showing Mary's increasing interactions, and March stretched far beyond the other columns. Her interactions were increasing in all categories.

We knew there were many reasons for Mary's wonderful progress. She was thriving in the small-class setting with an enthusiastic and dedicated teacher and aides. Also, she was receiving excellent speech and occupational therapy and learning in a progressive curriculum. Mary was working closely with her piano teacher, who was helping her stay on task and focused in her music, which had a carry-over effect to other areas of Mary's life. She also was well into the Rhinebeck program at this point, and the supplements were helping to lift the brain fog, allowing her teachers and therapists to have greater access to the real Mary.

At the parent-teacher conference in March, Mary's teacher showed us a video of Mary in her music class. The music teacher, off camera, sat at the piano and asked for a volunteer to lead the class in song. The camera showed all four kids sitting there for a few seconds, then Mary got up and said "I'll do it." The teacher started playing the piano and Mary started singing the song. It was one of those repetitive songs where someone sings a line, then the others all repeat it. This went on and on, back and forth, for about 15 lines of music. Mary sat in front of her class and teacher and correctly sang the entire song while using hand gestures that they had been taught to use with the song. Throughout the video, we saw Mary making eye contact with her peers, smiling, getting excited and having fun with the whole interactive experience.

I don't think I'll ever forget that moment. I can still see Mary leading the class in song with such confidence and enthusiasm. It wasn't a tear-jerker like the year before when she got up on stage at her other school and welcomed the crowd. That was a massive leap forward and a real surprise to us. This one was a positive affirmation that Mary was going to be OK, that she could lead others and be interactive, happy and enthusiastic all at the same time.

Mary breezed through the rest of the school year and continued to show academic progress as well as increased social skills. Very soon she would be off to first grade, back in the standard ASD Nest Program and on to bigger and better things.

23. Mary's First "Boyfriend"

Mary really blossomed in spring of her second Kindergarten year, and so did her affection for her classmate Ben. This was the same Ben she had seen every day for almost two years, first in the ASD Nest Program in Kindergarten at Castlewood Elementary then in the Intensive-K repeat Kindergarten class at Bergtraum Elementary. The first year, Mary barely mentioned Ben. On occasion Mary would say Ben's name in the context of something he had done at school that day, but she never really talked to us about Ben. But things changed in April 2008 when Ben and his mother Andrea car-pooled with Debby and Mary to a therapeutic horse-riding session on Long Island.

During the car ride to the horse camp, Mary and Ben sat next to each other in their booster seats in the back of the car. Debby said there wasn't much conversation, but Ben periodically pointed out various landmarks as they drove along. Ben has fair white skin and is lean, with short brown hair, often hidden beneath his favorite blue New York Mets baseball cap.

When they arrived at the horse camp, the lines were long and the wait was longer. It was also an unusually hot day, so after taking a turn brushing the horses, Mary, Debby, Ben and Andrea headed for the playground to have a snack. After about an hour, they went back to the stables and Mary and Ben each took a turn riding a horse around the ring. Shortly thereafter, everybody packed up to head for home, with Mary and Ben again enjoying the ride home together in the back seat.

When Debby reached Ben's house, Andrea invited Mary and Debby inside for an impromptu play date. Debby quickly agreed and the four of them spent an hour at Ben's house. Mary periodically asked Ben to join her in this or that activity, and there was a fair amount of interaction between them, even though much of it was non-verbal. After about an hour, Debby and Mary said goodbye and headed home, much to Mary's chagrin. She hoped to stay and play much longer at Ben's house, and all the way home she asked Debby when they could go back to Ben's house.

It amazed Debby and I that Mary became so attached to Ben. Up until that point, she never really had any true friends. There were many kids we had interacted with from her previous schools, and of course several kids in the neighborhood with whom Mary was familiar, but she never interacted much with them and rarely spoke to them. It was different with Ben though, and that was just the beginning.

Almost every day, Mary asked when Ben would be riding in the car with her again. Each time we got in the car, Mary would point over and say "that's where Ben sat." At the Intensive-K graduation ceremony, when all four Kindergarten classes were up on stage together, Mary sat right next to Ben. She sat there with her hand on his knee at least half of the time. The other half of the time Mary was folding Ben's hands for him or helping to guide him through the hand motions that accompanied the music.

A few days later was the 2008 Autism Walk in Manhattan, and Ben and his family walked along with our family. The attendance was announced as 11,000, so it was a crowded atmosphere. As soon as Mary saw Ben, she rushed over and grabbed his hand. She wasn't subtle about it either. Ben, who on occasion can be timid, didn't seem to mind at all. The two of them marched hand-in-hand the next two hours during the walk through the streets of lower Manhattan. They literally never let go of each other's hands for well over an hour at one point.

It was at that time that Debby and I and Ben's parents Jeff and Andrea started to joke around with each other that Mary seemed to have a boyfriend. At the young ages of 7 and 6, respectively, Ben and Mary certainly were too young to really think of each other as boyfriend and girlfriend. There was no doubting that Mary's feelings for Ben were unprecedented. She had never acted that way toward anybody despite much encouragement over the years.

The school year came to a close the following week and Mary kept asking when she would get to see Ben. We decided to set up a play date at our house, and Mary made sure that Ben sat next to her when we all had lunch. The two of them later jumped on the trampoline together, played several board games together and had a great time. The next day when we sat down to have breakfast, Mary pointed to the seat next to her and announced that that was Ben's seat. She reminds us of that fact every so often.

A week later, Ben and Andrea came back to our house for another play date and a visit to the public library around the corner. We all walked to the library together, although this time Mary took Ben's hand and put it in Andrea's hand, then she grabbed my hand and we walked hand-in-hand to the library. I guess Dad still rated! At the library, Mary picked up a book and thrust it at Ben.

"Here you go Ben," Mary exclaimed. "Read this one."

Ben reluctantly agreed, sitting down at the table across from Mary. A few minutes later Mary finished her book and picked out fresh books for the two of them. After that she went to the DVD section and found a few DVDs she liked, handing one to Ben. Ben didn't particularly like that DVD, but he grudgingly accepted it. This went on for almost an hour, with Mary finding books and DVDs for Ben and encouraging him to read the books or hold the DVDs.

On subsequent trips to the library, Mary pointed out where Ben had sat and what he did when we all visited the library together. The girl who rarely spoke to anyone for two years was finally learning to socialize, and it was wonderful and awkward at the same time. It was great to see Mary interacting with Ben and talking to him, but she didn't always quite know what to say. She was also somewhat forceful, unsure of how to "read" Ben's responses and reactions. For the most part, Ben accommodated Mary and went along with her quirkiness. Much of that accommodation I attributed to the many hours the two of them spent together the previous two years in school.

Debby and I were tremendously encouraged to see Mary forging a relationship with Ben. She asked about him and requested visits to see him very frequently. Then when they got together, she interacted with him, not 100% of the time but quite a bit. Though Ben went to a different school in a different program for first grade, we remained in regular contact with Ben and his parents who lived just 10 minutes away. Mary wouldn't be happy otherwise!

24. Steady Improvement for Mary

As Mary moved along with the Rhinebeck Health Center program, we saw new and wonderful developments in Mary all the time. She began reading books almost every night with Debby before going to bed, wonderful mother-daughter time that simply had not existed for many years. The books were getting more challenging and Mary kept right on progressing in her reading skills. Though full reading comprehension was still a ways off, Mary was getting much more proficient about sounding out words and reading well beyond the core sight words.

Mary's improvements were not limited to academics though. At Mass on Christmas morning in 2007, an usher asked our family to bring up the offertory gifts. Instead of cringing or politely declining, we accepted the honor. Debby and I immediately knelt down and asked

God for help, knowing that Mary would need to carry something up the aisle and stay with us, right during the middle of Mass, with dozens of people watching our every step. To our joy, Mary carried the basket of money and envelopes right up the aisle, walking with us stride for stride. She handed the basket to the priest, who commented how heavy the basket was and how strong Mary was to carry it there. She then followed us quietly back to our pew. She didn't run around on the altar or try to blow out the candles or refuse to give the basket to the priest or do anything improper. It was a proud moment for Debby and me, and we were sure that nobody in church that morning had any idea that Mary was anything other than a typical young girl. Nothing about her that morning said AUTISM or special-needs kid.

At a family party at Debby's father's house later that day, Mary rode her Aunt Melanie's wheelchair apparatus up and down the stairs several times. It's one of those contraptions that is attached to the side of the stairs to carry Debby's step-sister up and down the stairs since she has difficulty doing so on her own. When a few of Mary's cousins saw Mary riding up and down the stairs, they too became interested. Rather than run away from the sudden attention, or worse, become belligerent and refuse to share the ride, Mary instead chatted with her cousins for a few minutes and showed them how to work the electronics. She also organized the order of who would ride next. Mary repeated this aloud as a coping mechanism, forcing herself to share. It was a wonderful interaction because it occurred naturally and because Mary wanted it, not because she was told to say or do something.

We had plenty of fun over the Christmas holidays playing games such as Trouble, Candyland and Chutes and Ladders. Charlie enjoys games and previously when he asked to play, Mary usually ignored him or said she did not want to play. If she had played on previous occasions, it lasted a minute or two then she wandered off. But this time, Mary stayed and played several complete games. This happened on several occasions during the holiday break.

Later that winter we took the kids to an aquarium. The aquarium had many interesting attractions, but Mary especially wanted to try the SpongeBob Squarepants simulator ride. It's a moving ride where you enter a capsule, sit down and fasten your seat belt. As you watch the movie, the capsule jostles back and forth and up and down in sync with the movie. Because the movie was 3-D, we wore glasses to enhance the visual effects. On that day, Mary wore the glasses the entire time, fastened her own seat belt and enjoyed the whole experience. She laughed out loud a half-dozen times. Meanwhile, several other children were nearly in tears because they were scared. Not Mary, she loved every minute of it.

As winter finally neared an end, we signed Mary up for a children's yoga class. Courtney, the teacher, was an occupational therapist who enjoyed working with special needs children. The class was held in a small building, with a waiting area up front for parents and a yoga studio beyond that where the class was held. The first time there, Mary walked in like she owned the place, followed the instructions to remove her shoes and socks, carried her yoga mat into the studio and never looked back. From that point on, Mary was on her own. Debby waited in the front area of the building in the event that Mary did not stay with the class, but to our complete delight Mary emerged from the class at the end with the other students. Unlike previous years in gymnastics, where Mary was unable to follow instruction, she stayed on her mat and completed the yoga moves and never walked away or lost focus. She enjoyed the class tremendously.

Mary liked yoga so much that she took the opportunity to be the teacher during a break for the Easter holidays. We were home one day relaxing and Debby went out for a short run. When Debby got home, she started stretching on the carpet. Mary saw this and thought Debby was doing yoga. Mary walked over and said she would be the teacher!

For the next half hour, Mary told Debby what yoga poses to do and showed her how to do each one. They repeated the cycle a second time as well. Throughout the interaction, Mary made repeated eye contact with her mother and talked to her about each of the moves. Debby looked up halfway through and gave me the thumbs-up sign!

Recognizing that Mary needed to drastically improve her social abilities, we registered Mary for a Social Skills class at the local YMCA in the spring of her second Kindergarten year. The class brought together six young autistic children in a quiet setting. Each week the instructors, who were trained to work with autistic children, focused on an element of social interaction. The first week they concentrated on saying hello and saying something nice about a person when they meet them. The kids were given a short script to memorize as a guide to dealing with such interactions. The hope was that they would then use the script in a real-life situation when they met someone. At first the script sounded, well, scripted, but at least they had something to fall back on when they faced the situation of meeting someone.

The third week of class a new student joined the group, a 6-year-old girl named Brianna. She took a liking to Mary and the two of them talked to each other somewhat during the class exercises. We were pleased to see another girl in the class, since Mary was almost always the only girl in a class full of boys. Mary and Brianna sat together and ate snacks and started to form a bond as the class continued for a few weeks. Though not friends by any means, Mary and Brianna had each other to observe and talk to when they wanted. They played with similar toys and picked similar prizes when the class ended and it was time to exchange their good-behavior tokens for prizes. Once the school year ended in June, the social-skills class broke for the summer too. Mary continued with the social-skills class in the fall and throughout first and second grades, increasing her interactions with Brianna and her other young peers as well.

In Mary's first-grade class, which I will discuss in greater detail in Chapter 25, she was joined by two autistic girls, Makayla and Marissa. So after interacting almost exclusively with boy peers in pre-Kindergarten and her two years of Kindergarten, Mary was joined by other girls in both socials-skills and first-grade classes.

Debby and I knew it would be critical for Mary to develop relationships with girls. Whereas boys often get by with limited social skills by playing sports, Mary never showed much interest in sports and rarely played them. Though she loved dancing and singing, as of yet she hadn't shown the self-control to join a dance studio. That may be an option at some point in the near future, but even then Mary will need to interact with other girls and make conversations. The need to develop relationships with other girls will become even greater as she moves past childhood and into her teenage years, those challenging times when kids try to make sense of the world and of their own changing bodies. Having real girl friends she can talk to and have meaningful conversations with them should enable Mary to be more successful socially and to enjoy her teenage years more fully. So learning to interact with Brianna at the YMCA and with Makayla and Marissa in first grade was a great opportunity for Mary.

There were more immediate concerns though. There was still so much work to do. While we see Mary making progress every day, she reminds us of her special needs every day, too.

Not long after we moved into our new house in October 2007, Mary opened the back door, walked across the backyard and opened the gate. She walked right out of the yard and down the street. She walked around the corner and down a full block, along a busy street. She was gone only four or five minutes, but it terrified me when I realized she had left the yard. I initially thought she might be headed back to our old house or to our neighbor's house across the street from our old house, and I walked that way immediately.

As I started walking, I imagined the worst, picturing Mary lying in the street after getting hit by a car. Mary was known to cross the street without looking, despite being told 100 times to look both ways first, so it was possible. I quickly put that image out of my head and as I approached the busy street, I looked to my right and saw Mary a block down on the corner doing some kind of crazy dance move. A car had stopped to ask her if she needed help, and the woman had even called 9-1-1 because she was afraid Mary was lost.

I rushed over and hugged Mary for what seemed like an hour, then told the kind lady that Mary was my daughter and that she had autism and sometimes wandered off. She had never gone that far though, and all I could think about was getting her one of those medical ID bracelets with her name and phone number and the word Autism on it. Debby and I talked about the bracelets later that day but were hesitant to get one. On one hand they make good sense and could be critically helpful if Mary ever ran off again, but on the other hand we see getting her a bracelet as a sign of giving up. As long as we continue to care for Mary and teach her to be responsible, she may not need a bracelet after all. Mary knows the name of our town, street and phone number, and as her social skills improve, there is hope that if she ever does get lost she will just tell someone where she lives as well as her phone number. It's a debate we play out in our heads every so often.

We also continued to deal with Mary's obsessions with *Dora the Explorer* and *Sesame Street*. Over and over Debby and I tried introducing other toys and other television shows, but Mary kept going back to those old standbys. Over the summer before first grade she began asking for Barbie dolls and playing with more age-appropriate toys. Also, Mary continued to echo dialogue from computer games and television shows, although the intensity, duration and frequency of the echolalia was less than what it used to be. Dr. Mike thought this was a natural progression for Mary and that she would eventually grow past that stage, but it remained a challenge.

Mary continued to need priming before we tried anything new or different. Full-blown tantrums decreased substantially, but Mary still had mini-tantrums from time to time and needed redirection when she didn't get her way.

And while 7-8-year-olds aren't exactly renowned for their patience, Mary could be *extremely* impatient. She didn't tolerate waiting in lines very long and when she wanted something she would ask for it over and over and over again, as many as 10–12 times in 15 minutes, even though you had answered her question 10 times already and told her when she could expect what she was waiting for. And, like a 3-year old, Mary would walk over and do whatever came into her head when we were out somewhere. This might mean sitting down at the librarian's computer when she saw the seat was available or picking up another child's toy or personal belongings at the park even though the other child was right there using it. Very basic social cues just weren't there and needed to be continually spoken and reinforced, especially since Mary was so independent and self confident.

We didn't get much in the way of long conversations with Mary yet either, but there were signs that this was emerging. She was capable of answering a series of questions in a conversational tone, but her answers were usually choppy and sometimes off subject. Nevertheless, she would answer and interact for prolonged periods, which was a major improvement.

Mary's diet was a non-issue, something we all had become so accustomed to that we didn't worry much about it. But Mary herself didn't seem to grasp the importance of the diet yet. (This wouldn't develop for at least another year.) She couldn't see the big picture behind her diet, so when given an opportunity she would sneak something she was not supposed to eat and didn't really understand the repercussions. In time we expect she will embrace the diet and understand its importance and she will be the one to regulate her own diet.

Mary did learn to regulate her behavior when we got home from school each day. With precision, she would come through the door, take off her shoes and put them away, take off her backpack and hang it over her chair, take off her coat and hang it up with the other coats and then go to the bathroom. She did this every day because she was asked to do so. It was a routine that made sense to her and she wanted to behave appropriately.

She followed a similar routine after dinner. She would say, "excuse me from the table," then carry her plate and cup to the sink. She would then head upstairs and take off her clothes and put them into the clothes hamper. She picked out a pair of pajamas and carried them into the upstairs bathroom. She then went to the bathroom and waited for Debby or me to turn on the bath water. If we didn't come up there within a minute or two, she would call down to us to come help her. It was a highly effective and regular routine for Mary, something she did night after night.

By the end of summer 2008, Mary was a year into the Rhinebeck Health Program and a year into the GFCF diet. She was interacting more with her brothers and cousins and reading every chance she got. It was clear that she was well along on the road to recovery, but the next big test arrived in September when she started first grade. The academics were more challenging and the class size was much larger. Was Mary ready?

25. Stepping up to First Grade

We were quite happy that Mrs. Greene was to be Mary's first-grade teacher. Mary knowing her teacher so well and her teacher knowing Mary's quirks and motivators so well was a tremendous advantage when she took the leap from her self-contained, repeat Kindergarten class of four students to a first-grade class of 15 students. Mary also knew Derrick from her Kindergarten class because the two of them moved ahead into the first grade ASD Nest Program together. They were joined by the two autistic girls mentioned previously, Makayla and Marissa, and 11 other typical students.

The typical students were almost an even gender mix with 6 boys and 5 girls. We loved the fact that Mary would be in a class with 7 other girls! The question was whether Mary would retain the classroom discipline that Mrs. Greene and her assistants had instilled in the previous year. It was one thing to succeed in a class of four children; it would be another world altogether with 15 students and two teachers, and the last time Mary was in that setting at Castlewood things hadn't gone very well.

From the beginning of first grade Mary showed signs of adapting to her new class. She sat on the floor next to Derrick during the Morning Meeting as the class took attendance and discussed the calendar and weather. Mrs. Greene calmly helped keep her focused, either with a gentle caring rub on Mary's back or a verbal reminder whispered in her ear to pay attention. Small gestures and assistance from Mrs. Greene and her co-teacher, Mrs. Cecchetti, were helpful without question. And Mary was also helping herself, finally!

In her first year at Castlewood, Mary was undisciplined and unfocused. She had made remarkable progress in the next year and was able to follow along with the class by first grade. Her diet had improved dramatically to the point that she was no longer bloated, uncomfortable and spacey. The Rhinebeck program had removed many toxins from her body and corrected numerous nutritional deficiencies in her body, thus allowing Mary to think more clearly. The years of speech and occupational therapy had provided Mary with crucial stepping stones toward more appropriate language and motor skills. Her year of intensive Kindergarten had established the expected norms of a public-school classroom within Mary's head so she was keenly aware of what constituted appropriate and inappropriate behaviors.

As a result of all these interventions and years of work, Mary adapted quickly to the first-grade classroom. She no longer wandered off when non-preferred activities were scheduled, and she sat with the class and answered questions when called upon. After getting glowing reports from Mary's teachers the first few days, Debby and I finally exhaled. Sure the course work was going to be challenging, and Mary's behavior was far from perfect, but she was hanging in there finally! She could spend the day in a relatively large-class setting, surrounded by mostly typically developing students, and she could succeed. It was a tremendous relief for all of us.

It's a good thing Mary was adapting socially to the expectations of first grade, because the curriculum was challenging and the amount of work increased quite a bit compared to Kindergarten. Whereas in Kindergarten the students learned basic concepts of math and reading, in first grade things got much more specific. They had to read on their own and write weekly book reports (only a few sentences, but in their own writing accompanied by a drawing). They began adding and subtracting numbers higher than 10, requiring the use of a number grid at first since Mary only has 10 fingers to count on. They read sentences and deciphered simple math problems involving coins and dollars. In science they learned about solids, liquids and gases. There were weekly spelling tests, with challenging words such as "explain," "butterflies" and "hatching."

By mid-year, Mary's progress reports stated that she was at or near grade level in all subjects across the board and was expected to meet grade-level requirements by year end. Her reading, writing, math, science and physical-education skills were all very good and appropriate. The one area she was lacking was in social skills. She continued to show limited interest in conversations at school.

To spark more social interaction, Debby started putting short notes in Mary's lunch box each day. During lunch hour, the four autistic children ate together in the classroom early in the year while the rest of the class went to the cafeteria. Later in the year the autistic children also started going to the cafeteria at lunch hour for as long as they could endure the noise and distractions. However, despite knowing each other very well, the four didn't often have much to say during lunch hour. A swing teacher, Mrs. McCarthy, stayed with the four during lunch and helped guide them along. Upon seeing the notes from Debby in Mary's lunches, Mrs. McCarthy began reading the notes aloud and using them to stimulate conversations. The notes would often contain a reference to an activity Mary had scheduled later that day (soccer or piano) or would recap something Mary had done over the weekend (swimming at her cousin's house, jumping on the trampoline, etc.). The notes gave Mrs. McCarthy an insight into Mary's home life and helped jump-start some conversations amongst the children. It was a small step, but definitely one in the right direction.

In early January, Mary received a party invitation from one of the typical boys in the class. Jonathan, one of Mary's new first-grade friends, was going to celebrate his birthday party at a local bowling alley that the class had visited on a field trip earlier in the year. Jonathan's parents told him he could only invite a few people from school to the party in order to keep the party manageable, and Jonathan picked Mary as one of his invitees. When Mrs. Cecchetti and Mrs. Greene heard about this, they were giddy with excitement for Mary. We were pleased as well, knowing that Mary had started interacting enough, and appropriately enough, that a nice, typical boy she had only known a few months would invite her to his party.

It was with some nervous excitement and trepidation that we accepted the invitation and attended the party. For the previous few years, the only birthday parties Mary went to were family parties or parties of autistic classmates. In those instances Mary's quirks were tolerated unconditionally. At a party in a public bowling alley with predominantly typical children (in fact all of them were typical children as we found out), Mary's quirks would stick out like a sore thumb.

I prayed on the drive to the bowling alley that Mary would have fun and that she would just blend in and cooperate. The last thing I wanted her to do was run down an alley or throw a ball in the wrong direction or worse, throw some kind of tantrum. I didn't really expect any of that to happen, but I just didn't know. I did caution Mary to pay close attention to what the other children were doing and to wait her turn to bowl.

Mary and Jonathan were joined by about 10 other children, including about four others I recognized from Mary's class. They were spread out over three lanes and they all bowled a full game. Mary picked out a neon yellow ball that she liked and put it on the rack. She took a seat by the scorer's table and waited her turn. When Jonathan told her to go, Mary picked up her neon ball and rolled it (very slowly) down the lane. Other than some excited hand flapping as she watched the ball roll, Mary looked like a real pro up there and knocked down 7 pins. On her second shot she repeated the process and knocked down 1 more pin for an 8. She then calmly took her seat and watched the others bowl.

The whole time Mary bowled she followed protocol, used the same ball and had a great time. I prompted her on a few occasions to give high-fives to other bowlers after they made nice shots, and she jumped right up and did so. She did this once or twice on her own as well.

Following the bowling game, everyone headed to the party room for pizza and cake. I brought a gluten-free pizza and gluten-free cupcakes from home, anticipating the menu, and quietly substituted Mary's acceptable food for the party food. Nobody seemed to notice and Mary certainly didn't care. She ate her pizza, drank her apple juice then enjoyed her cupcakes.

When the group dispersed and started heading for the exit, I thanked the host and Mary said goodbye. As we walked to the car I thanked Mary for being so good and told her I was proud of her. I really was because she did an awesome job. When we got to the car, Mary buckled her seat belt and I sat down in the driver's seat. I took a deep breath, exhaled and smiled ear to ear. Mary was going to be OK.

Throughout first grade Mary started participating in organized sports through the YMCA. In the winter she played basketball in a program called Basketball Buddies, where autistic children were taught and coached by YMCA staff and a team of high-school-age volunteers. Most kids in the program had 1–2 high school "buddies" who helped show them how to dribble a basketball, to shoot baskets, to pass the ball, etc. For the first few weeks of the program, Mary churned through about four buddies before finally developing a rapport with buddies Maya and Molly. Mary started cooperating more and more each week with Maya especially, and enjoyed the routine. There was always a bit of stretching and jogging at first, followed by basic skills practice and then some shooting.

One of the benefits of Basketball Buddies was that Mary's classmates Makayla and Marissa also joined the program. The three of them would talk about Basketball Buddies at school and then see each other outside school each Thursday night. This helped develop a little bit of camaraderie between them.

Once Basketball Buddies concluded, most of the participants, coaches and buddies returned in the spring for Soccer Stars. It was the same concept in the same gym now focusing on indoor soccer. Maya and Mary once again teamed up and Mary learned to kick the ball, to pass it to others, to shoot the ball into the net and so forth. Mary's interest level seemed to fluctuate, both from week to week and within a session, but overall she enjoyed the sports and camaraderie there in the gym.

As the rest of the first-grade school year progressed, Mary continued to follow along with the class routines and kept up academically. As the math got more difficult, we worked together on the homework problems, started using flash cards to study and looked for opportunities to quiz her on the concepts. Each time there was an assessment, we were cautiously optimistic about Mary's chances. And each time, Mary passed the tests comfortably. Same thing was true in science and computers, where she had little trouble keeping up with the class.

Along the way Mary's writing also improved somewhat. In the beginning of the year her writing was crooked, meandering and sloppy. In the previous two years we were just happy to see her write down a decent answer. But in first grade we decided to hold Mary to a higher standard of penmanship, so in her homework assignments we required her to write more neatly. When she got sloppy, we erased her work and made her write it again. This led to a steady improvement in Mary's writing that the teachers noticed as well, although it remained very much a work in progress.

By the end of the school year in May 2009, it was time for Mary's IEP meeting to discuss second grade. There was no question in our mind that Mary was going to move up to second grade. We were pretty sure that she had behaved well enough to stay in the ASD Nest Program as well. During the IEP meeting Mary's teachers confirmed everything we felt. She was going to stay in the Nest program at that school, providing much needed consistency as this would be her third straight year at Bergtraum Elementary.

Her teachers had no serious concerns or issues with Mary, although they did allow in the IEP for Mary to continue receiving her tests 1-on-1 and with special accommodations and no timers. This would be critical for Mary going forward so she would be given every opportunity to demonstrate what she had learned in testing situations. At the end of the IEP meeting we all hugged and smiled and laughed. Mrs. Greene and Mrs. Cecchetti really cared about Mary and were ecstatic to see her improvement during the school year.

With Mary's IEP meeting out of the way and her school program set for the next year, we were just about due for another trip to Rhinebeck to see Dr. Mike. It already had been an exciting and adventurous year in Mary's Rhinebeck Healing Program, as I'll explain in the next chapter.

26. Hyperbaric Oxygen Therapy Helps

With Mary cruising along in late autumn of first grade, Dr. Mike thought it was time to step up Mary's healing program to include hyperbaric oxygen treatments. We didn't know much about hyperbaric oxygen therapy at that point, but we had heard a little bit about it. To be honest, it didn't seem that inviting. I knew it was expensive, first of all. And I couldn't picture Mary lying in a big tube with the sides all sealed off and oxygen flowing around her. I didn't think she would tolerate that kind of cramped environment. I didn't necessarily think she was claustrophobic, but I just didn't think she would go for it.

In addition to my doubts about Mary's willingness to cooperate was my skepticism that oxygen therapy would even help her. I had heard of celebrities visiting oxygen bars to feel and appear younger, but I thought that was a big con game. And if hyperbaric oxygen therapy was going to help Mary and be so successful, why had Dr. Mike waited well over a year into Mary's program to even suggest that we try it?

The more we thought about the doctor's suggestion and the more we researched the idea, the more it seemed like it was worth a shot. Dr. Mike had waited awhile to suggest hyperbaric oxygen therapy because he wanted to get Mary's other more pressing conditions under control first, such as removing the yeast overgrowth in her stomach and intestines and improving her overall vitamin and mineral levels. His thinking was that the hyperbaric oxygen therapy (HBOT) would help increase blood flow to Mary's brain, bringing oxygen to areas of the brain that may have been oxygen-deficient and not operating correctly. With increased oxygen levels and improved brain function, we hoped to bring about increased social interaction and verbal skills.

We discovered there were some parents in the autism community who thought hyperbaric oxygen therapy was the single biggest thing that helped their child recover. So in mid-December 2008 we found a hyperbaric oxygen treatment center located 20 minutes from our home. They required that Mary get a chest x-ray prior to starting the treatments, just to make sure she didn't have any deep congestion or pneumonia. With that taken care of, Mary started her oxygen treatments in late December. The treatments were expensive but we were willing to give them a try if they were really going to help speed us further along the road to recovery. Deep down inside I hoped that this treatment would be the big breakthrough, the one that would put us in the fast lane of the recovery autobahn.

An oxygen treatment session is called a "dive" because the tank is pressurized as if the patient was breathing oxygen while scuba diving. Inside the tank, the patient feels no real discomfort other than the pressurization one feels when flying in an airplane. Dr. Mike recommended that Mary take approximately 20-40 dives, with each taking an hour. This was going to be some time commitment! In fact, each dive would start with a 10-minute descent, until the pressure reached 1.3 ATA, then the pressure would level off and Mary would remain at that level for a full hour. After an hour, Mary would ascend slowly for 10 more minutes, so each session was actually an hour and 20 minutes, not to mention commuting time and the several minutes waiting for Mary to change into a hospital gown and to have her ears checked.

The hyperbaric technicians were always very cautious because oxygen is quite flammable. They did not allow patients to wear their own clothes into the tanks – everyone had to wear cotton hospital gowns inside. No jewelry was allowed inside the tanks either, for fear they might scratch against the bed frame or tube wall, spark and ignite the oxygen.

Debby and I had an orientation session one day while the kids were in school. We talked to the technicians and saw the tubes. They were about 8-feet long and made of glass. One end of the tube was sealed shut while the other end had a door that opened and closed like a cap on a tube of toothpaste. A hospital bed outside the tube could be slid forward to connect with the rails inside the glass tube, so the patient could climb onto the bed outside the tube and slide right into the tube on the bed. The technician would then disconnect the rolling bed frame and close the door with the patient inside. Mounted outside the tube was a television, which had speakers inside the tube. That way, patients could watch movies or television while breathing in the oxygen.

(This type of oxygen chamber is called a "hard chamber" because it's made of glass. It is capable of reaching higher oxygen levels than "soft chambers" that are made of a nylon-type material. The technicians told us that the hard chamber Mary used for her dives reached nearly 100% oxygen while soft chambers would only reach 20%–30% oxygen. The difference, we were told, was that hard chambers allowed for much faster progress in patients.)

So it was with some trepidation and nervousness that I took Mary to her first dive. She happily went along, knowing that she would be watching *Dora the Explorer* during the dive. We walked in and were handed a youth hospital gown, which Mary quickly changed into and hopped on the table. The technician checked her ears and made sure there were no infections or swelling of any kind. Then she took Mary's pulse and heart rate and everything checked out just fine.

With that, it was time to slide the bed into the glass tube. It was the moment of truth…would Mary cooperate? As the bed moved forward, Mary started flapping her hands.

"Daddy, daddy," she said frantically, her voice rising. "I'm here Daddy!"

I reached over and rubbed Mary's arm.

"It's OK Mary," I said. "This won't hurt at all. We just need you to lay back down and go inside the rocket ship. You can take the rocket ship to Dora's purple planet!"

I recalled an episode of *Dora the Explorer* where she went in a rocket ship to a purple planet to help some alien friends. For some reason at that instant I thought Mary might consider the hyperbaric oxygen tube to be a rocket ship. Amazingly, she smiled and said OK and laid back down. The technician slid the bed in, closed the door and we put the Dora video in the player. Mary looked around nervously for a minute, then gazed up at the television and that was that. She never banged on the glass to get out and she never panicked. When it was finally time to come out, Mary was ready but not anxious. All in all she handled the experience extremely well.

In the coming weeks, I observed about a dozen other young autism patients going on oxygen dives there too. All of the others went in the tube with a mother or father, but somehow we had gotten lucky and Mary was willing to go in by herself. That allowed me to read three novels over the course of her therapy as I sat outside the tube and waited for her!

We continued the dives for three months, going 2–3 times per week. Mary would come home from school at 2:30 p.m. and relax for awhile, then we'd tackle her homework. After homework, she had a little more time to relax before having an early dinner. Then it was off to oxygen therapy, usually from 6 p.m. to 7:30 p.m., and finally back home by 8 p.m., just in time for a bath and bedtime. It was definitely a grind for both of us, not to mention for Debby taking care of the boys at home, but we felt it would be well worth it if Mary showed progress.

And boy did Mary ever show progress! This therapy really worked for Mary. After just 8 or 9 dives, Mary started commenting about things that she saw. She would say things like "Daddy, you're wearing a striped shirt today," or, "Charlie ate all of his french fries." These were basic observations that she was making, but the difference was that all of a sudden she was sharing them verbally; perhaps all of these years she was noticing our shirts and seeing how much we were eating but just never saying anything. I'm sure she was! It was exciting to hear her sharing her thoughts suddenly.

Also, Mary started commenting about things she saw as we were driving. For years she had sat numbly in her car seat when we drove anywhere, but now she started commenting.

"Whee, this is like a roller coaster," Mary exclaimed one day as we drove down a sharp, curving hill on the way to the hyperbaric center. From that point on she announced "roller coaster" every time we approached that curve.

We also noticed that Mary was having short conversations with us finally. We could ask a series of questions and get a series of answers. This held true even if the questions were somewhat vague, such as "What did you do at lunchtime at school today?" Such a question previously would have gone unanswered 99% of the time, with the rare answer being something such as "we played." Now Mary would tell us whom she ate lunch with and even share a few details of what they ate or what kind of games they played after eating or whatever. We were finally getting a glimpse into Mary's day!

About 25 dives into Mary's treatments, we had a bit of a scare one night. Mary was in the tube watching a movie when the technician thought she smelled gas. At first I didn't smell anything, then I did notice a faint gas smell. She decided to shut off the oxygen just to be safe, not knowing where the smell was coming from and what caused it. I was initially irritated because Mary was only 20 minutes into the dive and now we'd have to go home and had barely gotten any help that day.

However, looking back I'm glad we played it safe that day. In early May, 2009, I read a CBS News report online about a 4-year old boy in Florida who was receiving hyperbaric oxygen treatments for Cerebral Palsy. The boy was in the tube with his grandmother and the pressure was very high, possibly as high as 1.7 ATA. (Recall that Mary's oxygen never went past 1.3.) For some reason, the oxygen ignited in the tube and the boy and his grandmother were covered in flames. They were rushed to the hospital but were burned on 90% of their bodies. Such a horrific accident is not common and was at least initially blamed on a technician error. Nevertheless, it was a terrible and tragic accident that underscores the risks involved with this treatment.

By the time we heard about the hyperbaric accident in Florida, Mary was already done with her dives. She finished 36 dives in all and we believe they were a tremendous success. We never told anyone at her school that she was getting those treatments, and we were happy to hear the teachers commenting that Mary was talking more in class and participating more often.

Interestingly, in November 2009, research conducted by the Center for Autism and Related Disorders, Inc. found that HBOT therapy does not have a significant effect on symptoms of autism. A double-blind, placebo-controlled trial found that there was no significant difference in autism symptoms between the groups. Both direct observational measures of behaviors symptomatic of autism and standardized psychological assessments were used to evaluate the effects of the treatment.

Nevertheless, like so many other families, we observed improvements in Mary that simply cannot be downplayed, ignored or attributed other than to the hyperbaric oxygen treatments. The HBOT therapy led to Mary making more observational comments than ever before, a welcome improvement in our household. No, the HBOT therapy didn't cure Mary by any means, but I absolutely believe it helped push her along the road to recovery.

With the hyperbaric oxygen treatments concluded, it was time for another step in Mary's healing program. This time Dr. Mike recommended that Mary begin glutathione injections to help further detoxify her body. In his book *Healing the New Childhood Epidemics,* Dr. Bock says, "Glutathione is now one of the Big Guns in the biomedical arsenal against autism." Dr. Mike shares Dr. Bock's embrace of glutathione, which Dr. Mike said could help speed Mary along in the detoxification process. He explained that glutathione would detoxify the heavy metals in Mary's body and help rid her of other toxins as well. In addition, the glutathione should stop free-radical damage that was harming Mary. Dr. Mike explained a number of other more technical benefits of glutathione, which are also detailed in *Healing the New Childhood Epidemics.*

The very day that Dr. Mike told us about the glutathione, we walked over to the nursing station and they set Mary up with a glutathione IV drip. Fortunately Mary never minded needles, whether giving blood or in this case the IV drip. The IV took a half hour, then we relaxed for a half hour to make sure Mary handled the treatment well. She did, and off we went.

Mary returned two more times for glutathione IV drips over the next 4-5 weeks, with the glutathione level increased each time. After the first two sessions we didn't notice much difference in Mary, but after the third session she was really weepy and emotional for a few days. Clearly something was stirring in her and emotions were bubbling to the surface. This was both exciting and troubling, because Mary was learning to deal with emotions at age 7 that most children had learned to at least somewhat manage long ago. The fog and haze in Mary's brain and in her world was lifting further, and she was dealing with reality more and more.

Mary got her weeping back in check after a few days. However, we observed that Mary still hadn't learned to control her emotions. No longer giddy and spacey all the time, Mary became irritable at times depending on the circumstances. She would sit and play nicely with her brothers, even talking to them and interacting regularly, but if they got too noisy or irritated her in some way she would instantly get upset and lash out at them. She might slap them, throw a toy at them or pinch them, depending on her mood. What she really needed to learn was to tell them to quiet down, to use her words to get them to stop goofing around or bothering her. She just didn't have the speaking skills developed enough to convey her thoughts, so she began responding physically to them.

A similar phenomenon occurred whenever Mary got bumped accidentally. If someone stepped on her foot or bumped into her, even if barely hard enough to only slightly hurt, Mary began overreacting. She didn't understand the concept of an accident, that if someone bumped into her in the hallway at school that it wasn't on purpose. The person could apologize immediately but Mary would still get sidetracked. She would mumble the phrase "no cupcakes for Mary," apparently relating her immediate pain and anger to the deeply felt sorrow that she associated with being told at some point in her life that she wasn't going to get a cupcake. When that cupcake experience happened we weren't sure, but it obviously impacted Mary. For several months Mary continued to overreact to getting bumped, mumbling "no cupcakes for Mary" and lashing out at the person who bumped her.

We discussed Mary's emotional fragility with Dr. Mike and he said it sounded like Mary was having trouble understanding other people's feelings and intentions, another part of her social development that needed to be mastered. It was good that she was finally reacting and interacting with others he said, but she needed to better understand how the other person felt, especially if they were apologizing.

A few weeks after her third IV Mary had another glutathione IV and she handled it well. She didn't get weepy or particularly emotional afterwards. Once school started again in the fall we put the IV treatments on hold, but in December, 2009, Dr. Mike suggested it was time to move Mary further along in the detoxification process and we began IV chelation (key-lay-shun). Mary received calcium-EDTA in a slow IV drip, followed by the glutathione. The intention was for this to continue for two months, with the goal of removing Mary's heavy metal toxic burden, primarily lead, aluminum and mercury. (Prior to starting chelation, Mary was tested for heavy metals and her levels of lead, mercury and aluminum were all very high.)

Unfortunately, some of the side effects of chelation are irritability and hyperactivity, and Mary exhibited both immediately. Her teachers commented that she was difficult, unfocused and irritable the three days immediately following the first chelation appointment, so we decided to postpone further treatments until summer 2010 so that any side effects would not be detrimental to her schoolwork.

Starting and stopping various treatments and strategies can be frustrating, but we have been determined to do all we can to help Mary. She's a work in progress that may take awhile to solve. The road forward in Mary's recovery can be bumpy and challenging at times, but as long as we feel like we're moving forward overall we just keep at it and work with Mary and her team of therapists and educators to bring out the best in her.

27. Challenging Second Grade Curriculum

We were happy and delighted for Mary to continue on to second grade within the ASD Nest Program at Bergtraum Elementary in the fall of 2009. For the first time in two years, Mary would have a new teacher, two in fact. Fortunately, one of the teachers would be Mrs. McCarthy, whom Mary already knew from first grade. Mrs. McCarthy was the swing teacher for the Nest program in 2008-2009 who I mentioned used to read Mary's notes from Debby at lunch time to help spark conversation. Mrs. McCarthy also took the kids to classes outside the usual classroom, such as computers, science and physical education. She worked with Mary just about every day in first grade, then also worked as one of the summer-school teachers. By the time second grade started Mary and Mrs. McCarthy were long familiar with each other. Joining Mrs. McCarthy as the second-grade Nest teacher was Mrs. Mashriqi, an enthusiastic young lady with experience teaching first through third graders. They would be assisted on a regular basis by an energetic third teacher, Ms. Webb, who usually ate lunch with Mary and encouraged her to comment on her meal, her day so far or anything else Mary cared to talk about.

Mary and her Nest friends were now part of a large and growing population of children thriving within the school district's ASD Nest Program. According to a school district brochure, the ASD Nest program started in September 2003 at a school in Brooklyn with nine children on the autism spectrum. From such a humble beginning, the program grew quickly. By September 2009, the Department of Education had opened an additional 13 ASD Nest elementary programs throughout New York City, serving approximately 225 autistic children in the program. There was also a middle-school program in Brooklyn and a high-school program in Queens.

Now higher-functioning autistic children in New York City fortunate enough to gain entry into the ASD Nest Program can look forward to an integrated education program from pre-Kindergarten through high school. It's amazing that when Mary was turning 2, the program was only in its first few weeks, with less than 10 children on board, and by the time she turned 8 there were more than 200 children attending Nest classes at 16 different schools citywide!

If there's one thing we learned about the ASD Nest Program in the past three years though, it's that the children have to learn, grow and also meet certain promotional criteria to keep moving forward in the program. It can be a bit stressful at times, because there's always this underlying feeling that a few bad weeks could wreck your child's standing within the program and cause him or her to get sent out of the Nest, which would likely be followed by a mad scramble to find some sort of suitable replacement. Mary learned that after her first year of Kindergarten, when her out-of-seat behavior and foggy brain caused her to lose her spot in the regular Nest class for a year while attending the new Intensive-K option.

Mary's academic and behavioral development progressed nicely from the time she started in the Intensive-K class, and as detailed in Chapter 25, first grade came and went successfully. Next it was time for second grade, a year with higher expectations and a rising of the bar for Mary's development.

On the first day of second grade, Mary looked around the room and saw many familiar and friendly faces. That had to be comforting for her. Her three friends on the spectrum from first grade, Makayla, Marissa and Derrick, were all joining her in the second-grade classroom. Most of the typical students that filled out the class were also from the first-grade Nest class, so Mary had to feel secure and confident in her surroundings from day one of second grade. Debby and I were overjoyed at the consistency that was becoming part of Mary's education.

For Mary's 8th birthday in late September, we visited the classroom and brought gluten-free cupcakes and apple juice for the class. Debby asked Mary to pass out the treats to her friends, and Mary took the tray and walked desk to desk handing them out. "Here you go," she would say to each person, including the correct name each time. Mary did a great job and didn't need any help at all. She then walked around and handed out the juice boxes before taking a seat at her own desk. The whole class sang "Happy Birthday" to Mary, who smiled along happily. When the song ended, Mary prompted the kids to continue.

"Are you 1?" Mary asked aloud. "Are you 2?"

The whole class picked up on it and asked if Mary was 3, 4, 5, 6, 7, then finally 8. Mary didn't answer right away, and the whole class hesitated.

"I am 8," Mary finally declared, and the whole class clapped with joy.

It was a great way to start the school year. As the weeks went by, Mary breezed through the homework and had little trouble keeping up with most of the school work. Some of the early work was more or less review from the end of first grade, and Mary's teachers used many of the same homework formats from first grade so that Mary quickly followed along with the program without any major transitional difficulties.

However, it was noted that Mary's reading comprehension was not improving quickly enough. She could read and sound out words pretty well, but she was speeding through the books and not really taking time to understand what she was reading. In second grade, Mary needed to be able to understand what the characters were thinking, feeling and doing. Reading comprehension quickly became a major concern, and in December we hired a tutor to work with Mary twice a week on reading comprehension.

Math was a different story. One of the first things we did was work with the teachers to wean Mary off of the number grid for solving basic addition and subtraction problems. In first grade, Mary had mastered the number grid and could add or subtract by "hopping" forward or backward the appropriate number of spaces to solve the problem. That was a nice baseline to fall back on, but in second grade, Mary needed to be able to solve simple problems (e.g. 7+11= __ or 13-9= __) quickly and on her own rather than pulling out a number grid every time.

To solve these problems, the teachers taught Mary to take the first number and put it in her head as the starting point. Mary was literally to touch her forehead and say the first number. She would then either add or subtract the second number depending on the problem. Mary picked up on this very quickly and we were able to move forward without the number grid within the first few weeks of school.

Unfortunately, as second grade progressed Mary continued to show trouble with anger management. This had started toward the end of first grade when Mary started reacting physically when she would get bumped accidentally. First Mary would say "no cupcakes for Mary" and become upset. Soon she started saying "no cupcakes for Mary" or "no cookies for Mary" and become upset then pinch or slap somebody. Usually it was her brothers Charlie or Marty who were the victims, but it started happening at school and at her Social Skills class occasionally too. It was not an everyday occurrence, but it happened frequently enough that Mary's teachers, Debby and I became greatly concerned.

To address the issue, the teachers began scheduling regular breaks for Mary so she could relax for a few minutes in a quiet corner of the room. She was also only given about 4 items on the schedule at a given time, thus she did not have to see and comprehend a lengthier schedule of activities. Also, unfortunately, Mary had to continue eating lunch in the classroom while most of her classmates were eating in the crowded and noisy cafeteria.

At home, we bought several books about sensory integration. We pulled out a book called *Meghan's World*, by Diane M. Renna[16], that Debby had received from a mother/author in 2008 whom she met on the return bus ride from the march for greener vaccines in Washington, D.C. The book was about a girl with sensory integration problems who utilized the Wilbarger Brushing Protocol to help overcome some of her sensory challenges.

The brushing protocol, developed by occupational therapist Patricia Wilbarger, utilizes a small surgical brush that is rubbed with firm pressure on the arms, back and legs. Following the brushing, the child receives joint compression treatments on the shoulders, elbows, wrists, hips, knees and ankles. This is all done within five minutes and is performed three times per day in most cases. The goal of the brushing method is to lessen a child's sensory integration difficulties and widen her sensory comfort zone. The child's behavior is potentially more predictable and calmer, leading to less pent-up frustration and anxiety, which ideally means far fewer outbursts. While not a magic cure, it can be a key part of an overall recovery program especially in kids who have sensory issues. Because rare but serious side effects can occur with brushing, our occupational therapist recommended that parents should always consult with a trained occupational therapist before starting the program.

With much optimism and hope, we set up an appointment with our private occupational therapist in Whitestone for early November. The session went well from the very first minute. When the therapist introduced herself to Mary, Mary looked right at her and responded.

"Hi, how are you?" Mary asked.

I nearly fell over. I don't think I had ever heard Mary respond so quickly, appropriately and correctly without any prompting from me whatsoever. That was a good omen. We went inside the office and the therapist mentioned that she personally had learned to manage her own sensory integration challenges earlier in her life and now worked to help others. Within five minutes she described Mary's behaviors almost exactly and demonstrated a keen understanding of Mary's sensory challenges. It was enlightening and encouraging right away.

The occupational therapist calmly talked to Mary about the brushing method and what she was going to do. She then asked Mary if she could brush her arms and Mary agreed. She repeated this for every step of the process and made sure I saw how to do it. Mary not only tolerated the brushing and joint compression but seemed to really enjoy it! She giggled at times and never once tried to pull away. This pleased the therapist, because she said some kids have zero tolerance for brushing and won't cooperate. When she finished, the therapist then had me take the brush and brush her arms, then had me try the joint compression movements as well. Once satisfied that I was adequately trained, she wished us luck and sent us on our way. We were to continue the brushing method at home three-times daily and meet with her in a month to ascertain if the method was working.

The early results on the brushing were promising. Mary had a great day at school, then it was off to the dentist for a cleaning. That's just how the schedule worked out, first brushing on Tuesday then to the dentist for a cleaning on Wednesday. Previous trips to the dentist did not go well. When Mary was 4-6 years old she would sit on my lap and I would hold her arms down as the dentist cleaned her teeth. It was always a struggle and Mary never cooperated for long. As she got stronger, that no longer worked and for several visits they had to give Mary gas to temporarily sedate her during the visit. I was prepared for more of the same on this occasion.

After I picked Mary up from school, we came home and went through the brushing routine. Then we jumped on the backyard trampoline with Charlie and Marty for 10 minutes, then it was time to go see the dentist. When it was Mary's turn, she climbed right into the chair and let the dentist put the napkin around her neck. She then let him recline the chair and she opened her mouth wide and said "aaaaaaah." It was perfect, but there was a ways to go.

Mary actually allowed the dentist to put an x-ray card in her mouth and she bit down. I stood behind her and held her chin shut, which she didn't fight. We then took a second x-ray and again she was relaxed and easy. Mary tolerated the dentist lightly scraping her teeth, then she picked the chocolate flavored toothpaste for the brushing/cleaning. Still no gas, no arm restraints, nothing! Mary squirmed a little during the brushing but stayed in the chair. When that was done, the dentist inserted a fluoride container in Mary's mouth and asked her to bite down on it. Mary did and we talked softly for about three minutes while Mary bit down in the fluoride. When that was done, we were done! No screaming, no kicking, no swinging her arms, no crying and best of all, no gas. Oh, and she had no cavities either! How much Mary's cooperation was attributable to the therapy brushing we'll never really know, but it was an immediate positive sign for us.

While the long-term success of the brushing was yet to be determined, we were hopeful that it would lead to a reduction in Mary's anxiety and sensory integration problems. If she became less sensitive to getting bumped or nudged, she would have fewer aggressive outbursts and more success in school and in her activities. The occupational therapist also told us several other good techniques for stress reduction. One was to have Mary clasp her hands together tightly in front of her whenever she got frustrated or excited, instead of flapping or waving her arms. This would help her center and calm herself instead of releasing energy randomly and peripherally. Also, the therapist recommended that Mary be told to squeeze her own arm when she felt frustration or rage building, so she could release the negative energy safely and painlessly on her own arm instead of hurting herself or someone else. We happily accepted these tips and put them to use right away.

Unfortunately, in addition to some anger management issues Mary was not always comfortable with the class size of 15 students. Her teachers said prior to beginning the brushing, Mary often tensed up when the class returned from a break. The large number of children and associated noises and distraction bothered Mary. In November, when report cards were sent home, Mary was given a "promotion in doubt" notice from the school. That was disappointing of course, and was due partially to Mary's anger management issues and anxiety in class. For two months she was uptight at times, lashing out whenever she got frustrated. The brushing helped soothe Mary immediately, and it made her once again more open to teaching and learning. The occupational therapist at Mary's school commented in early December that the Mary of the past few weeks, after starting the brushing, was a totally different Mary than the child she saw the first two months of the year. Just a few weeks after the brushing treatments started, in fact, Mary had a major math test and she aced it, getting the highest possible score.

The ASD Nest Program team devised a behavior intervention for Mary beginning in January 2010 that showed immediate promise. Mary was given a laminated letter-sized chart with enough space to write three activities, thus breaking down the larger daily class schedule into a more manageable subset for Mary. The first three activities on the class schedule were written on Mary's card with a dry-erase marker. Other basic expectations, such as listening to the speaker, being quiet and being nice, and where Mary was to sit, were also written on the card. Toward the right side of the chart was space for either a happy face if Mary completed the task correctly or a frowning face if she did not complete it correctly. Next to that was the final column noting if Mary would get a small reward or not. Each time Mary completed a task correctly, she was given a quick reward, such as a few minutes with a favorite book or using a small toy. The rewards were kept in a nearby empty desk. Her teachers noted that Mary was given about two minutes per reward because it was during that two-minute period between scheduled tasks that Mary's focus often drifted and/or she engaged in negative behavior. Having a reward during those transition times helped Mary bridge the gap successfully between activities.

Initially, the teachers had to write out each activity on the schedule card, with appropriate expectations noted. However, within a week, Mary was so in tune with the program that she started looking up at the schedule board in front of the class and writing her own personal schedule on her card. The teachers were happy to see this because it showed Mary taking ownership in the process and requiring less one-on-one assistance, which was a big step forward in regulating her own behavior.

Another component of this intervention was a second laminated card, which had the word COMPUTER at the top, then the numbers 5, 4, 3, 2 and 1 descending vertically, then the words NO COMPUTER at the bottom. Each time Mary was not nice in class, if she pinched or pushed somebody, the teacher erased a number. If they erased all five numbers before lunch time, Mary would not get free computer time during lunch break. Through the first three weeks of the program Mary had not missed a day of computer time. She was determined to self-regulate in order to get that computer time.

Right away the new intervention worked. In addition to not losing any computer time, Mary improved her behavior during routine tasks and began focusing much better on those tasks, according to her teachers. Mary was so motivated for the little rewards that she began regulating her behavior immediately and her negative reactions toward others significantly decreased.

The schedule intervention worked really well for about six weeks, then Mary started to grow tired of the reinforcers. She also started showing some aggressive behavior again at times, pushing classmates and occasionally throwing things in class. Though nobody was hurt by this, the reversal in Mary's behavior was disappointing to her teachers and family. Mrs. McCarthy revised the schedule to include a wider variety of reinforcers for Mary to choose from, and we added some new toys from home to encourage Mary to comply.

Nevertheless, Mary's school principal and the ASD Nest team decided that Mary had reached a critical point where she was requiring too much individualized attention. Though she was doing well academically, Mary's inconsistent behavior was also a concern. As a result, in early March 2010 the ASD Nest team informed us that Mary would need a new placement in the fall. She would have to proceed with third grade at a different school. The ASD Nest team recommended that Mary be placed in a smaller class setting where she could get more individualized attention and achieve greater success.

While Debby and I were disappointed to be wrapping up our four-year stay in the ASD Nest Program, we looked back with great satisfaction and appreciation. Mary's academic abilities in spring 2010 were far beyond where she was when she started the program in Kindergarten in 2006. Though her social skills were lagging, Mary's ability to follow class routines, complete school work, comprehend reading and compute math problems were all at or nearly at grade level as she concluded second grade.

Our next challenge would be to find the next "right" learning environment for Mary. We immediate began a search of local schools. Fortunately, New York has a wealth of special education schools. However, finding the right spot for Mary would take some time. Meanwhile, we had a more pressing challenge to tackle at church.

As Catholics, second grade has significant meaning to us as well, because Mary was preparing to make her First Holy Communion at Holy Trinity in spring 2010. Fortunately, the second-grade religion teacher's assistant at Holy Trinity had a background in special education and was helping Mary along the path to that important First Communion. Mary had to memorize several traditional prayers, learn about the contents of the altar area in church and comprehend the significance of Holy Communion. The religious education administrator for Holy Trinity provided Debby and I with supporting materials to use when working with Mary at home to reinforce the principles taught in the classroom each Sunday morning. She also let us know that gluten-free Eucharist would be available to accommodate Mary's special needs. Mary's godmother Rachel retrieved her daughter Lindsey's beautiful white dress that she wore for her First Communion in 2007 and gave it to Debby so Mary could wear the same dress that her cousin wore on her big day.

Mary's First Communion will further deepen the bond between Mary and the church, following Mary's baptism there, her critical preschool intervention at the Whitestone School within Holy Trinity's elementary school and, of course, her religious education classes. Holy Trinity has been part of Mary's life from the beginning, and as she moves along her road to autism recovery, we find ourselves continually fueled by the prayers and support of the Holy Trinity community.

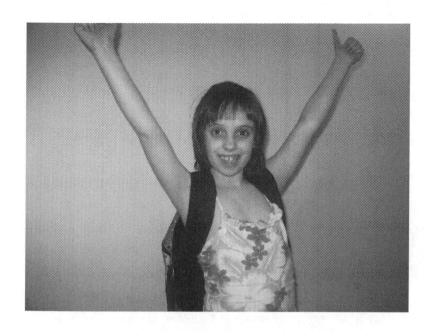

28. Triumphant At Last!

We spent much of the summer of 2009 at the Bay Terrace pool club in nearby Bayside, Queens. Mary was excited that we purchased a summer membership to swim at the club. Sometimes I thought she was the real Little Mermaid, the way she loved to swim. Given that Mary and Charlie had each completed several years of swimming lessons, I was confident that I could watch 2-year old Marty and teach him to swim while keeping an eye on Mary and Charlie with help from the lifeguards.

My biggest concern about the pool club was not the kids' safety in the water but the logistics of getting all three kids out of the pool, dressed in dry clothes and back to the minivan again all by myself. (Most days we went to the pool in the afternoon while Debby was working.) Getting there was easy – we put on swim suits at home and when we got to the pool Mary and Charlie went in on their own. Getting out of the pool and drying off and changing clothes was a much greater challenge!

For one thing, Mary's lack of social awareness meant it was quite possible that she could get out of the pool and just take her swim suit off in front of a few hundred people. Second, she never announced when she was done swimming. I had to constantly keep one eye on Mary from across the pool so I would know when she was ready to go. Then when I saw Mary getting out of the pool I would scoop up Marty and notify Charlie that it was time to go. There was no discussing this with Mary. When she was done, that was it, and we all had to go.

That's when it would get awkward. I didn't think it was possible for me to send Mary into the women's locker room on her own to dry off and get dressed. It just would never work. And I certainly couldn't go into the women's locker room with her! Unfortunately, the only Family changing room was small, stacked full of supplies and usually locked. There was no way I could corral three youngsters while carrying towels and a clothes bag while tracking down someone with a key to that room. I would have had better luck juggling chain saws while tap dancing! Leaving the club without changing would mean walking back to the car in wet swim suits, which Mary simply would not tolerate. That left one option: Mary had to come with us into the men's locker room.

By that time, Mary was nearly 8-years old, 4-feet tall, 55 pounds and not a little girl at all. Bringing her into the men's locker room was uncomfortable. Nobody ever complained about us, at least not to our knowledge, but for five days a week for six weeks, I felt uncomfortable and awkward every time. I would quickly help Mary peel off her wet suit, then hold up a towel while she dried herself off. She then got herself dressed while I frantically dried off the other two boys and myself. It was chaos for five minutes every time.

After about six weeks of this routine, we came on a weekend with Debby. When we were done swimming, Debby took Mary to the women's locker room while I helped the boys get dressed. It was much more peaceful and relaxing for everyone. The next day however, I was back at it again on my own with the kids when I saw Mary get out of the pool. Charlie was nearby taking a tennis lesson on the club's courts, so I quickly made my way across the water to help Mary. But I was too late. As I climbed out of the pool with Marty I saw Mary walk into the women's locker room. Uh-oh. Panic time.

I couldn't send Marty in after her; he wasn't old enough to go on his own. And I couldn't walk away and pull Charlie out of his lesson to help, because I was afraid Mary would come prancing out of the locker room naked at any moment. I was just going to have to figure something out. I stood there for a good 6-8 minutes outside the door, wondering what to do as I watched for Mary to come out again. Suddenly I heard an announcement: "WILL RANDY ROBERTSON PLEASE COME TO FIRST AID?" My heart skipped a beat, but I knew someone in the locker room must have connected Mary to me and called for help.

In fact, a pool club employee saw Mary talking to herself in the nude in front of a mirror in the locker room, her wet swimsuit on the floor. When asked, Mary was able to tell the pool club girl her name and that she was there with her Dad. The girl then found my name on the computer and called for me. When I arrived, the girl discreetly said that Mary couldn't find her clothes. She then asked if I had Mary's dry clothes. I handed her the bag and a few minutes later they both came out. I thanked the girl and she then told me what had happened. I was glad that Mary responded to her questions and that it all worked out OK.

When I asked Mary why she went in there by herself, she pointed to the sign that read "WOMEN'S LOCKER ROOM" and said that she wanted to go into the *women's* locker room. All this time perhaps she had been uncomfortable in the men's locker room too, but hadn't found a way to express herself. Finally she just went in to the women's locker room on her own, since she is perfectly capable of reading the sign and had already been in there with Debby.

At that point I knew there was no going back to the men's locker room for Mary. I was going to have to trust Mary to get dressed on her own. Before we went back to the pool club the next day, we packed Mary's dry clothes in her own bag. I told her that she could go to the women's locker room again, but she had to bring her bag in with her and get dressed on her own. We discussed this about six times before we left the house and Mary nodded and said "OK" each time.

When we got out of the pool that day, I handed Mary her clothes bag and a dry towel and sent her off on her own into the women's locker room. I didn't know what to expect, but I hoped for the best. After about eight minutes, Mary came walking out...dressed! However, she didn't have the bag or the towel or her wet swimsuit. I asked her to go back and get them, and after a few minutes she came back with the bag but not the swimsuit or towel. I was half pleased and somewhat irritated to have to ask again, but Mary said she couldn't find her swim suit. I sent Charlie in and he came back in a minute with the swimsuit and towel. That was a pretty good first attempt, but we had to get better.

The next day, before leaving for the pool club, Mary and I went over the changing routine again. This time I stressed the importance of putting her wet swimsuit and towel into the bag once she was dressed and bringing everything back out with her. Then off we went to the pool and had a great time swimming for an hour. Right on cue, Mary got out of the pool when she was done and headed for our towels. I followed right along and handed her the clothes bag and some last minute instruction reminders. Mary said "OK, Dad" and walked into the women's locker room.

This time, Mary came out in just five minutes. She was fully dressed and had her clothes bag over her shoulder. She looked right at me and walked over with a smile on her face. Before I could say anything, she proclaimed "I did it, Daddy!"

I gave her a huge hug and didn't want to let go.

"You sure did," I said proudly. "Great job, Mary!"

And from that day forward Mary went into the women's locker room on her own to get dressed. No more awkward trips to the men's locker room. No more running off on her own and wandering around naked. She now responsibly takes care of herself after swimming just like most other 8-year-old girls do.

I will always remember the elation both Mary and I felt when she first went in on her own and got dressed alone and came back to meet us successfully. She was proud of herself too, and we both recognized that this was a major milestone and achievement. It meant even more to me that she was able to verbally communicate her happiness in completing this task. At that moment if felt like autism was 1,000 miles away. Mary was just a regular girl.

This new development not only made the rest of the trips to the pool club easier for all of us, it boosted my spirits in the big picture of things, too. Mary was growing up and starting to take care of herself. It was a minor task for her to get dressed at the pool club, but there were several steps involved and she did them all on her own successfully and with pride. That showed me that Mary has the intelligence and determination to succeed on her own, and that's an incredibly uplifting and powerful feeling. It's a feeling that our whole family and extended circle of friends and support team worked very hard to achieve. Mary's autism recovery is not complete, but week by week, little by little, we really are finding Mary, and it's wonderful.

Tips for Parents of Autistic Children

Finding Mary has been an amazing, grueling and frustrating journey, but it's all we know. And now that we're making real progress, finding Mary is becoming more interesting and enjoyable by the day.

As our journey to find Mary enters its fifth year (and counting), we look back and thank God for all of the progress Mary has made already. Mary reads and sings and talks to us again, and she seems genuinely happy. She has had to work for that progress, as we all have, these past few years. Along the way we have come to know so many special people who are making a difference.

We also know that we are among the fortunate ones. No two children on the autism spectrum are alike, and Mary sits on the more high-functioning side of the spectrum. For all of the struggles and challenges we have faced, we know there are families facing more serious challenges and disabilities and our hearts and prayers go out to every one of them. And while this book focuses on a child with autism, due to our own personal experience and the recent surge in autism diagnoses, we are well aware that there are thousands of adults with autism that are suffering and/or dealing with challenging circumstances every day. Autism is all day, every day and it wears you out. We now know that we are fortunate though because Mary does communicate and speak and is making such incredible progress.

It seems only appropriate to conclude with a summary of the major factors that have helped us. This is not a cure-all for autism, because sadly there is no cure for it. Autism is so varied and unique to each individual that no simple, step-by-step solution exists. However, I believe the following 10 factors should be seriously considered by all families facing the autism challenge.

1. **Pray for help.** Do this continually and openly. Ask for miracles, and in fact visualize them happening. See it in your mind and believe it. Never underestimate the power of prayer and positive imaging. We had tremendous success with the Novena to St. Joseph, a powerful nine-day devotion with a specific goal requested.

2. **Read books about autism to better understand the disability**. I personally found *Overcoming Autism: Finding the Answers, Strategies and Hope that can Transform a Child's Life* by Lynn Kern Koegel and Claire LaZebnik and *Healing the New Childhood Epidemics: Autism, ADHD, Asthma and Allergies* by Kenneth Bock, M.D. and Cameron Stauth to be incredibly powerful and motivating.

3. **Try a strict gluten-free and casein-free diet for at least three months.** We put off trying this for two years and regret waiting so long. Mary showed immediate improvements in her sleep, bowel movements, energy levels and awareness just by making this one change. It's not easy making the change, but there are many gluten-free substitutes out there and the rewards are well worth the trouble.

4. **Assemble a team to help you achieve your goals**. This sounds daunting at first, but there are many wonderful speech, behavioral and occupational therapists out there. Seek out schools and school programs that help provide a team framework for your child. Constantly evaluate your team, what impact they are having and make changes if necessary.

5. **Advocate on behalf of your child.** Obtain all of the necessary services from the school district during the IEP (Individual Education Program) process and be firm. Be aware of what is needed for your child to succeed. As you progress from year to year, be careful about reducing services if you believe they are still necessary. Be cooperative and partner with your school district to achieve what is best for your child.

6. **Use picture schedules to establish routines.** The effectiveness or necessity of this factor will vary from child to child, but most autistic children we have met and known have thrived when using picture schedules. They help provide order and security to the day. As kids progress and develop, engage them in the schedule process and let them help determine the schedule when appropriate.

7. **Use timers to ease transitions.** Mary likes routines, doesn't like surprises and she doesn't like being suddenly moved from one activity to another. Give her a heads up, set a timer, and she'll agree to most anything. She would sit and play computer games for an hour and if I came in and said OK, let's turn this off now she would be upset and perhaps throw a tantrum. If, however, I let her play for 30 minutes then set a timer and told her 5 more minutes, she would hear that timer beeping then shut the computer down herself without having to be asked twice. It's amazing how effective timers are for some kids.

8. **Prime the child before doing something new or potentially undesirable.** Mary doesn't always like loud noises or crowds, but if she knows about them ahead of time and can start dealing with them mentally before facing them, she does much better. It's similar in concept to the picture schedule, in that if she knows what is coming, she's better prepared to handle it successfully. This is true for all of us really, but even more critical for children on the autism spectrum.

9. **Don't be afraid to try "alternative" treatments with supervision.** There are few globally accepted and medically proven autism treatments out there. Instead there are tons of strategies that have been used with varying degrees of success. I highly recommend locating a Defeat Autism Now! (DAN!) doctor in your area and seeing what he or she suggests. Not everyone believes DAN! doctors are correct, but the successful anecdotal evidence is overwhelming. Mary is a perfect example of a child thriving under the care of a DAN! doctor. For example, we hesitated to try the gluten-free, casein-free diet for too long. Once we understood that Mary has imbalances in her body that can be easily corrected through supplements, we jumped at the chance to try it. The results have been excellent to date. We also found success using Hyperbaric Oxygen treatments and the Wilbarger Brushing Protocol, again in each case with the assistance of licensed professionals.

10. **Spend as much quality time with your children as possible to understand them and their abilities.** All kids have abilities and things that make them happy. Find out what makes your child happiest and cherish those moments you have together. We found that Mary loves music, especially dancing around and playing the piano. She also loves playing duck-duck-goose and computer games. We use computer games as a reward for achieving academic goals. Instead of dwelling on her short-comings, we look for opportunities for Mary to make music and have fun.

References

(1)   In the December 18, 2009 issue of *Morbidity and Mortality Weekly Report*, the U.S. Centers for Disease Control (CDC) stated that autism now affects 1 in 110 American children. Further, the CDC stated that 1 in 70 American boys are diagnosed with autism. Autism Speaks, the advocacy organization, estimated that based on this new data nearly 750,000 American children are now on the autism spectrum, an increase of 600 percent in the past 20 years. (www.autismspeaks.org)

(2)   Albuterol is a bronchodilator that relaxes muscles in the airways and increases air flow to the lungs, according to the website Drugs. com (see http://www.drugs.com/albuterol.html).

(3)   Corticosteroids are a class of steroid hormones produced in the adrenal cortex. Corticosteroids are involved in a wide range of physiologic systems such as stress response, immune response, and regulation of inflammation, according to the website Wikipedia. See: http://en.wikipedia.org/wiki/Corticosteroid

(4)   *When the Moon is High*, Alice Schertle, HarperCollins Publishers, 2003. All of our kids loved this book with its beautiful illustrations, especially Mary.

(5)   *Overcoming Autism: Finding the Answers, Strategies and Hope that can Transform a Child's Life,* Lynn Kern Koegel and Claire LaZebnik, Penguin Books, 2005.

(6)   The Individuals with Disabilities Education Act (IDEA) is a law ensuring services to children with disabilities throughout the nation. IDEA governs how states and public agencies provide early intervention, special education and related services to more than 6.5 million eligible infants, toddlers, children and youth with disabilities, according to the government website. See website at http://idea.ed.gov/ .

(7)   A SEIT, or Special Education Itinerant Teacher, provides assistance to students in addition to the education and therapy the child receives in the classroom. For example, in New York state, related SEIT services "include, but are not limited to, speech-language pathology, audiology, interpreting services, psychological services, physical therapy, occupational therapy, counseling services (including rehabilitation counseling), orientation and mobility services, evaluative and diagnostic medical services to determine if a student has a medically related disability, parent counseling and training, school health services, school social work, assistive technology services, appropriate access to recreation, including therapeutic recreation, other appropriate developmental or corrective support services, and other appropriate support services and includes the early identification and assessment of disabling conditions in students," according to the Statewide Coordinator for Special Education. See website at http://www.vesid.nysed.gov/specialed/publications/preschool/seit.htm

(8)   According to Autism Speaks, "hundreds of published studies have shown that specific ABA techniques can help individuals with autism learn specific skills, such as how to communicate, develop relationships, play, care for themselves, learn in school, succeed at work, and participate fully and productively in family and community activities, regardless of their age." Autism Speaks notes that ABA therapy should be customized for each individual and recommends that it is designed and overseen by a qualified,

well-trained professional behavioral analyst. See website at: http://www.autismspeaks.org/treatment/aba.php

(9) The TEACCH Autism Program is a division of the University of North Carolina Department of Psychiatry. According to its website, "TEACCH is an evidence-based service, training, and research program for individuals of all ages and skill levels with autism spectrum disorders. Established in the early 1970s by Eric Schopler and colleagues, the TEACCH program has worked with thousands of individuals with autism spectrum disorders and their families. TEACCH provides clinical services such as diagnostic evaluations, parent training and parent support groups, social play and recreation groups, individual counseling for higher-functioning clients, and supported employment. In addition, TEACCH conducts training nationally and internationally and provides consultation for teachers, residential care providers, and other professionals from a variety of disciplines. Research activities include psychological, educational, and biomedical studies. The administrative headquarters of the TEACCH program are in Chapel Hill, North Carolina. See website at: http://teacch.com/

(10) The Autism Nest Program has been growing steadily in New York City's public schools for the past six years. For more specific information see the New York City Department of Education website at: http://schools.nyc.gov/Academics/SpecialEducation/SchoolImprovement/Projects/OtherProjects/About_ASD.htm

(11) The Global Advisory Committee on Vaccine Safety in 2003 concluded that no evidence exists of a causal association between MMR vaccine and autism. See World Health Organization website at: http://www.who.int/vaccine_safety/topics/mmr/mmr_autism/en/index.html In addition, the Centers for Disease Control on its website lists several studies that show no link between the MMR vaccine and autism. See website at: http://www.cdc.gov/vaccinesafety/Vaccines/MMR/MMR.html

(12) The gluten-free, casein-free diet really helped Mary, but first we had to learn what gluten and casein were and where to find them. For a good overview of what gluten and casein are, try the WebMD website at: http://www.webmd.com/brain/autism/gluten-free-casein-free-diets-for-autism and for a word of caution before starting the diet see the Autism Speaks website at http://www.autismspeaks.org/treatment/associated biological medical conditions.php

(13) For a great read on biomedical treatment of autism, I highly recommend *Healing the New Childhood Epidemics: Autism, ADHD, Asthma and Allergies* by Kenneth Bock, M.D. and Cameron Stauth, Ballantine Books, 2007. The authors go into great detail about various probable causes of autism, ADHD, asthma and allergies and provide many treatment options, all of which should be considered only under the direct guidance of a medical professional.

(14) *Teach Your Child to Read in 100 Easy Lessons* by Siegfried Engelmann, Phyllis Haddox and Elaine Brruner (Fireside, 1986). This is a great book for teaching youngsters to read. Both our typically developing sons and our autistic daughter made it through the lessons successfully.

(15) The Defeat Autism Now! project of the Autism Research Institute is described in greater detail at the ARI website: http://www.autism.com/index.asp . The site includes recovery videos, parent testimonials, a list of clinicians and much more. It's a very useful and encouraging site.

(16) *Meghans World*, by Diane M. Renna, Indigo Impressions, 2007.

It has become a family tradition to complete the Autism Speaks Walk Now for Autism event in Lower Manhattan each June. We've done it the past three years and plan to continue for years to come.

In appreciation for all that Autism Speaks has done to raise awareness of autism and promote research, I am donating 10% of all author proceeds from "Finding Mary: One Family's Journey on the Road to Autism Recovery" to Autism Speaks.